Civil War Stories

of northwest ohio heroes

photography & narrative by

Jim Mollenkopf

CIVIL WAR STORIES

of northwest ohio heroes

photography & narrative by
JIM MOLLENKOPF

©2002 Lake of the Cat Publishing,
P.O. Box 351454, Toledo, Ohio, 43635-1454
ISBN 0-9665910-3-8
Library of Congress Control No. 2002111479

First Edition
Second printing, September, 2005

Table of Contents:

List of Illustrations & Photographs

Foreword

Dawn lay a couple of hours away in Charleston Harbor in South Carolina on April 12th, 1861 when the roar of cannons shattered the morning quiet as the Confederate bombardment of Fort Sumter gave the thunderous news that a long-simmering Civil War had begun. That thunder would rumble for four long years, echoing across the country, northwest Ohio included.

Tens of thousands of soldiers from northwest Ohio went off to that war. The men and boys that went included husbands, fathers, sons, brothers, fiancees, friends, and boyhood pals. They came from the cities of the area such as Toledo, Findlay, Lima and Sandusky as well as the region's villages and farms. They ranged from privates to generals; from drummer boys to spies.

Most were volunteers, fighting for something in which they believed. Their experiences were recorded in what is at best a patchwork of official records, regimental histories, diaries, letters and post-war reminiscences, some of which are included in this book. Stories in this book include:

- The 21st Ohio Volunteer Infantry out of Findlay and its heroic defensive stand at the Battle of Chickamauga.
- Two Wood County members of the Andrews Raiders who survived hellish months both in prison and on the run after their fabled, but failed, raid.
- The 111th Ohio Volunteer Infantry out of Toledo which

fought in over 20 battles and endured one harrowing night where the regiment nearly ended up at the bottom of the ocean.

- The Confederate prisoner of war camp on Johnson's Island in Sandusky Bay, where thousands of prisoners sat out the war, including one unrepentant young rebel who had grown up just a few miles away.

- The 38th Ohio Volunteer Infantry out of Williams and Defiance counties which kept its colors flying during a fierce Georgia battle, but at a high cost.

- A captain from Napoleon who spent a year at the death camp that was the notorious prison at Andersonville, Georgia and lived to tell about it.

- Major General James B. McPherson of Clyde who was the highest ranking Union officer killed in the Civil War.

- Legendary northwest Ohio editor David Ross Locke whose fictional Petroleum V. Nasby character skewered the South and amused the North, including troops in the field and Abraham Lincoln in the White House.

- Toledo Congressman James M. Ashley, an abolitionist who during the war walked the political point in pursuit of legislation banning slavery.

- Young John Kountz of Maumee who began the war as a humble drummer boy, achieved fame during it, and gained national repute afterward.

On the cover of the book is the painting, *Battery H, First Ohio Light Artillery In Action At Cold Harbor, Virginia, June 3 and 4, 1864*, painted by the famed 19th and early 20th century military and figure artist Gilbert Gaul—the majority of the original soldiers and subsequent recruits of Battery H were from Toledo and Lucas County. Organized in the fall of 1861, it served through the end of the war fighting in 13 battles and numerous skirmishes and sieges.

After the war members of Battery H decided they wanted to leave behind a unique memorial. The painting of the battery in action at Cold Harbor, Virginia, was commissioned in the late 1880's and took Gilbert Gaul about two years to complete and was submitted to military critique and examination during its preparation. The painting is considered to be of high historical authenticity and faces of the soldiers portrayed are believed to be of the actual members of Battery H. The battery left no record, however, as to why it chose Cold Harbor which was, for the Union, a particularly brutal defeat.

The large painting with gilded frame was displayed at the World's Fair in Chicago in 1893 and had its Toledo unveiling in an 1894 ceremony. There, keynote speaker Governor William McKinley of Ohio called it "a striking picture of the war, a picture which for all time will be a memorial to the splendid services of Battery H." He also called it a tribute the common soldier, "these men who did the great work of the war."

The painting was then on display in old Memorial Hall in Toledo before being given by surviving members of the battery to the Toledo Museum of Art in 1915. In later years it was displayed at the Toledo Zoo and at some point in time was placed in storage under less than ideal conditions.

The painting was transferred to the Oregon-Jerusalem Historical Society in Oregon, Ohio in 1989. There it was obvious that time and the elements had not been kind to the painting and a costly restoration would be needed. Due to the efforts of the society the restoration returning the Gilbert Gaul work to its original glory was completed in 2002. Now the painting can once again fully provide a look back to a moment frozen in time in that great and terrible drama that was the Civil War.

The full 8-foot by 5-foot painting of Battery H can be seen at Brandville School, an 1882 schoolhouse and museum owned and operated by the Oregon-Jerusalem Historical Society, 1133 Grasser St., Oregon, OH 43616, 419-693-7052.

Author's Note: The following organizations were of particular help in providing material for this work: the Oregon-Jerusalem Historical Society; The Allen County Historical Society in Lima; the Williams County Historical Society in Montpelier; the Rutherford B. Hayes Presidential Center in Fremont; the local history and genealogy department of The Toledo-Lucas County Public Library; Sandusky Library and the Center for Archival Collections at Bowling Green State University. In addition the historical journal *Northwest Oho Quarterly* was a valuable resource as it has been in my previous books.

If the Civil War could be described as a movie of epic length, this work is but a few frames. It is not, nor is it intended to be, a full presentation of the northwestern Ohio experience in the Civil War. Historic and reference data for such an effort do not exist and even if it did, such a work would require volumes.

In working on this book I discovered that my great-great-grandfather, John Mollenkopf of Maumee, fought in the Civil War. He was a blacksmith and a recent immigrant from Germany when the war started. In the summer of 1861 he left his wife and two young children behind, one my great-grandfather, and traveled to Cleveland to join the 37th Ohio Volunteer Infantry, a German-speaking regiment. A sergeant, he served through the end of the war. He was a member of the same company as John Kountz, the drummer boy from Maumee whose story appears in this book.

DEDICATION:
To Sergeant John Mollenkopf
Company G, 37th Ohio Volunteer Infantry

CHAPTER I

OHIO IN THE WAR

During the four years of the Civil War the Federal government asked Ohio for over 306,000 men, a number which the state exceeded by four thousand. Ohio ranked third among states in numbers sent, behind only New York and Pennsylvania, although it was first in proportion to its overall population. Approximately 60% of all Ohio males between the ages of 18 and 45 served.

They suffered and died in an almost unbelievable variety of ways although, as on a national basis, disease was by far the number one killer. Statistics compiled after the war showed that 35,475 Ohio soldiers died. Of that number 21,721 succumbed to disease, 6,835 died in battle, and 4,753 died of battle wounds. The fourth leading cause of death, 784, was by drowning. The rest perished in other types of accidents and of a variety of causes both unknown and known including murder, execution, suicide and sunstroke.

When the war started numerous military camps for organizing regiments were hastily built in cities and towns across the state such as Camp Toledo in Toledo, Camp Vance in Findlay, and Camp Lima in Lima. Most were temporary and short-lived. Camp Dennison in Cincinnati and Camp Chase in Columbus were major military camps, the latter having a large prison for Confederate soldiers as well.

The predominant Civil War military unit was the infantry

regiment and Ohio raised nearly 200 of them. Regimental organization continued through the war and soldiers from a given geographical area could end up in a range of units. For example soldiers from lightly populated Sandusky County in northwest Ohio served in 25 different infantry regiments, four cavalry regiments, three Ohio National Guard units, as well as a number of artillery batteries.

An infantry regiment was composed of ten companies of about 100 men each including officers. The companies were lettered alphabetically A through K. The letter J was historically not used by the army as it resembled the letter I too closely when written. A regiment had an authorized maximum strength of around 1,025 although once on the march, attrition from disease and battle was rapid. For example the average Union regimental strength at the Battle of Chickamauga in September, 1863 was 440.

At Chickamauga, which was the bloodiest two-day battle of the war, Ohio soldiers comprised about 30% of the Union's Army of the Cumberland. Of the 44 infantry regiments from Ohio, 15 lost more than 100 men while two lost more than 200. In total nearly 5,000 men from the Buckeye state were killed, wounded, or captured.

The first ever recipients of the Congressional Medal of Honor, six surviving members of the Andrews Raiders, were from Ohio. A total of 143 Ohioans were awarded the medal for valor during the war. And five Ohio Civil War officers, Ulysses S. Grant; Rutherford B. Hayes; James A. Garfield; Benjamin Harrison and William McKinley went on to be presidents of the United States.

CHAPTER II

Major General James B. Steedman

At the corner of Summit and Galena streets in Toledo stands a soldier, hand resting on sword, and bronzed in time. That soldier is Major General James Blair Steedman, a onetime Toledoan, and the only Toledo veteran so honored with the casting of a statue.

Born in 1817 in Pennsylvania, he faced his first major life challenge at the age of 13 when a scarlet fever epidemic killed his parents on consecutive days. Responsible now for himself and three siblings, he left school and became an apprentice printer. After a few years of this he got his first taste of the military, joining Sam Houston's campaign for the independence of Texas.

He returned to Pennsylvania and ran a gang of canal workers for a time and in 1838 followed the canal boom west to Ohio and Napoleon. He landed a contract to build a section of the Miami and Erie Canal near Waterville and was challenged to a fight by a blacksmith working on the project who told Steedman that if he wanted to stay in Ohio, he would first have beat him in a fight. The brawl went on for nearly three hours, so the story goes, with only Steedman standing at the end. The blacksmith would never fight again.

While living in Napoleon he became involved in the newspaper business as well establishing *The Northwest Democrat* in upriver Defiance. In the 1840's he served a couple of terms in the state house of representatives and the year 1849 found him in California chasing gold in that state's gold rush. The 1850's found him living in Toledo where he continued his involvement in Democratic politics and printing, eventually rising to the prestigious and lucrative position of public printer under President James Buchanan. A sharp disagreement with Buchanan over Stephen A. Douglas, of whom Steedman was a loyal supporter, led to the end of that position.

Major General James B. Steedman was Toledo's highest ranking Civil War officer. (National Archives).

In 1860 he ran and lost a close race for the U.S. House of Representatives to the abolitionist James M. Ashley, Steedman's hands-off views on slavery probably costing him the election. And when the Civil War broke out in April, 1861 the well-known Steedman, who was a major general in the Ohio militia at the time, was a natural to lead a local regiment. Within days the 14th Ohio Volunteer Infantry from Toledo and other northwest Ohio towns had been raised and by April 25th were off to Camp Taylor in Cleveland with Colonel Steedman at the command.

Colonel Steedman and the 14th Ohio wasted little time as they were among the earliest troops to move into Confederate territory. They fought in the first land battle of the Civil War at Phillipi, Virginia in early June where a force of 2,000 Confederates was routed, the 14th being the first Ohio regiment to unfurl its colors in battle. When the regiment's three-month term of service expired, Steedman and his men returned to Toledo to a hero's welcome and were again mustered, this time for a three-year hitch. Colonel Steedman and the 14th Ohio were fighting again by October.

By August, 1862 Steedman had been promoted to brigadier general, now in charge of a brigade. For his actions in the Battle of Chickamauga in September, 1863 he was promoted to major general. His troops honored him there as well, giving him the nickname "Old Chickamauga." Even those who disliked him personally gave him credit for his battlefield prowess. A colonel who served under him claimed he paid inadequate attention to the physical needs of his men and that "his devotion to cards and whiskey and women filled the measure of his delight except when under fire, and then he was a lion."

In early December, 1864 he rushed troops to Nashville as the Confederates were menacing that city. His regiments were of both white and black soldiers, the latter having yet seen battle. Under orders to make a feint to distract Confederate attention from the main point of attack, Steedman drove the Confederates back over half a mile and captured two lines of earthworks. The Battle of Nashville went on to become a smashing Union victory.

After the battle General Steedman said, ""The question is settled; Negroes will fight." He later wrote in his report, "I was unable to discover that color made any difference in the fighting of my troops. All, white and black, nobly did their duty as soldiers." When the war ended in April, 1865 he was named military governor of Georgia, one of only two non-West Pointers named to such a high position. He was also involved in other postwar administrative duties before retiring from military life in August, 1866.

Steedman's service had elevated his status from that of locally-known journalist and politician to that of a figure of national repute. He remained in public life, serving as collector of internal revenue for the city of New Orleans from 1867 to 1869. He returned to Toledo and jumped back into local politics and served as editor of the *Northwest Ohio Democrat*.

In 1878 Steedman, then a 61-year-old widower, raised local eyebrows when he married 16 year-old Mildred Gildea. That same year he won a term to the state senate and in 1880 was delegate to the Democratic National Convention. In the spring of 1883 he was elected Toledo's chief of police but this would be his last role. In October that year he died of pneumonia at the age of 66 and, after an elaborate funeral attended by thousands and during which schools and businesses closed, was buried in Toledo's Woodlawn Cemetery. His young wife never remarried and lived until 1948.

The statue erected in his honor did not come from a great outpouring of public sentiment but rather was the gift of an old friend, a Toledo brewer Steedman had befriended back during his canal days. The bronze statue with its Vermont marble base was dedicated in May, 1887 at the corner of Summit and Cherry streets in downtown Toledo. It was moved to its present location in 1920. There the old general gazes forever south, toward the former Confederacy, almost as if keeping an eye on his onetime adversary.

This statue of General James B. Steedman stands at the intersection of Summit and Galena streets in Toledo. Carrick's Ford was the first battle he fought in while a colonel in command of the 14th O.V.I. mustered in Toledo. The other battles inscribed are Chickamauga, Perryville, and Nashville.

CHAPTER III

NORTHWEST OHIO & THE BATTLE
OF CHICKAMAUGA

Summer was in its annual melt to fall in the latter part September, 1863 and there probably was no prettier place to witness this splendor than the Cumberland Mountains in northwestern Georgia near the Tennessee state line. Craggy peaks swept down to river-lined valleys as majestic forests, touched with early autumn color, reached for the blue sky.

And tens of thousands were there, not for the autumn vistas but Union and Confederate soldiers with a grim task at hand. It had not been a good summer for the South with disastrous defeats at Gettysburg and Vicksburg in early July. As the summer wore on the Union set its sights on Eastern Tennessee and the key rail center of Chattanooga, for control of that city would open a route to Atlanta and the heart of the Confederacy.

As the northern Army of the Cumberland continued its advance on the city, the Confederates, under General Braxton Bragg, withdrew from Chattanooga in early September to defensive positions in the hills and gorges of the Cumberlands, preferring this to the possibility of being surrounded in the city. The Northerners, under General William Rosecrans followed. By the third weekend in September the two sides were lined up high above a creek called the Chickamauga, said to be Cherokee for "river of death." And at dawn on the 19th a battle exploded that would become the bloodiest two-day fight of the Civil War.

Unlike many previous battles in which armies generally met on open terrain, the rugged hills and forests of the region made for a somewhat confusing clash. Commanders at times could only guess where the enemy or their own troops were. Battle lines surged back and forth. Territory was captured, lost, and recaptured, some several times over.

When night fell over a long day's fighting that had ended generally in a stalemate, the sounds of battle were replaced by the pitiful sounds of the wounded moaning and begging for help. The temperature plunged and soldiers on both sides lay on the ground shivering, both from the cold and from a haunting chorus of human suffering.

On Sunday the 20th the battle resumed. And it was on this day that the 21st Ohio Volunteer Infantry out of Findlay and General James B. Steedman of Toledo, in separate units, and both of which had seen little action the first day, would rise to prominence.

The 21st O.V.I. at Chickamauga

The 21st Ohio Volunteer Infantry was drawn primarily from the rural areas of Hancock, Wood, Defiance, Ottawa and Putnam counties. They came both from farms and sprouting towns such as Findlay, Defiance, Perrysburg, Elmore and Ottawa, men and boys headed into harm's way. The majority of them were farmers and sons of farmers according to a regimental captain were generally, "peaceful, quiet, industrious, intelligent, and self-reliant, and not contaminated by the follies and vices of city life."

Originally mustered in Findlay for a three-month hitch in April, 1861, most came back to Findlay where the regiment was reorganized for three years of service in September, 1861. Between November, 1861 and March, 1865 the 21st Ohio would fight in at least 22 battles and numerous lesser skirmishes.

Of the many battles in which the 21st Ohio fought, the largest was the Battle of Chickamauga. It was also where the regiment stood its tallest. For there in what has been called one the heroic defensive stands of the entire Civil War, the northwestern Ohio soldiers played a significant part in preventing a Union defeat from becoming an annihilation, one that could have lengthened the war.

Around mid-morning on the 20th as the battle raged, Union General Rosecrans made a major tactical error. Perceiving there was a gap in the Union line where there in fact was none, he ordered a major movement of troops to fill the perceived breach and, in the process, created a real one. The Confederates just happened to be launching a major attack against this weakened point and before long, several rebel divisions poured through. The result for the Union was catastrophic.

U.S. Assistant Secretary of War Charles A. Dana, napping at General Rosecrans' command post after getting little sleep the previous two nights, awoke to a tumult. Seeing the devoutly Catholic general crossing himself, he knew there was a problem. He then leaped to his horse and in astonishment "saw our lines break and melt away like leaves in the wind." The better part of five Union divisions were suddenly in chaotic retreat north toward Chattanooga, most converging on a single pass called McFarland's Gap. Along the road to the gap was a crush of frightened soldiers and accompanying horses, wagons, and artillery. The wounded limped and staggered along as best they could, many collapsing alongside the road to die. If the Confederates were able to cut off the retreat the number of Union killed, wounded or captured would be enormous.

But the battle was not over. A portion of Union troops, under General George Thomas, were standing firm and were fighting furiously in an area called Snodgrass Hill, from the south and west of which extended a series of small hills and ridges that came to be known collectively as Horseshoe Ridge. In the aftermath of the collapse of the Union line, General Thomas had re-positioned his troops and now stood in a generally east-to-west line between the Confederates to the south and the Union troops who were fleeing to the north. One of the regiments fighting under General Thomas that day included the 21st Ohio which was positioned along Horseshoe Ridge.

The 21st Ohio, a veteran regiment of 539 men under the command of Lieutenant Colonel Dwella Stoughton, had more than experience going for it. Seven of the regiment's ten companies had been recently equipped with a revolutionary new weapon: Colt repeating rifles with five-shot cylinders, patterned after the pistol. The gun, while a bit slow to load, could deliver five shots in as little as nine seconds. And each soldier was well stocked with nearly 100 rounds of ammunition.

By early afternoon the 21st Ohio, which was holding the far

right of General Thomas' battle line, was engaged in a furious fight, Lieutenant Colonel Stoughton having already gone down with what would prove to be a mortal wound. It had been a dry summer and the fusillade unleashed by both sides ignited the undergrowth causing brush fires, burning some of the wounded of the regiment as they lay helpless on the ground. A young second lieutenant from Findlay, seventeen-year-old William Vance or "the boy" to the other men, was thrust into command of Company D when its captain was wounded. Of that hellish day he later wrote, "Volunteers rushed forward and drew the poor fellows back but some of them were piteously burned, the white, cooked, flesh peeling back from their charred finger bones, and in the case of an old school-mate of mine, great flakes falling off his cheeks. And so they died."

The fight raged on, the outnumbered men of the 21st frequently letting the Confederates advance near before unleashing a deadly hail of bullets. The rebel charges "were so continuous they might be almost counted as one," according to Lieutenant Vance. On many occasions "the pressure seemed intolerable and not to be resisted any longer, when the heart would almost give way, and the brain was fairly paralyzed at the thought that, after all, we must yield." Yet on they held.

Sergeant John Bolton of the 21st Ohio wrote, "we hold our fire until they are again close upon us...the rapid firing from our repeating rifles at short range is terribly destructive and again they waiver for a moment when their columns begin to wither away and soon again disappear." During one of these volleys a terrified Confederate soldier dropped his rifle and bolted to the line of the 21st Ohio and surrendered. Stunned to see only a single line of men he exclaimed "My God, we thought you had a whole division here!"

As the battle continued, the roar of the gunfire, the tremendous number of casualties, and the smoke from the gunpowder and brush fires created a nightmarish scene. And a few of the men of the 21st Ohio began to crack under the strain as described by Lieutenant Vance. One soldier ran out in front of the line ranting, raving and firing at the enemy while turning to curse his colleagues for not following. No amount of commands or coaxing could convince him to return. He continued in this way until a Confederate bullet permanently stilled his rage.

Another, after part of his hand was shot away, erupted in dancing, gyrating, profanity, refusing to go the rear. Unable to load his weapon with his damaged hand he sought the assistance of a wounded comrade who, though lying on the ground, could still load a gun. He kept firing and yelling until he fainted from the loss of blood.

Horseshoe Ridge as it appears today with a monument honoring the 21st Ohio. The ridge is part of the Chickamauga and Chattanooga National Military Park.

Yet another soldier was found by Lieutenant Vance laying face down behind a tree. When he asked him what was wrong the soldier babbled "I'm wounded. I'm wounded," while pointing to a spot on his forehead where there was obviously no wound. Lieutenant Vance ordered him to return to his position and the soldier refused to budge. Finally the lieutenant, despite the fact that the man was more than twice his age and nearly twice his size, lost his temper and struck him several times with his sword, finally driving him back to his position where he resumed firing.

About ten minutes later Lieutenant Vance came along the line and found the soldier lying on the ground, his lifeless eyes staring upward. "He was dead," he wrote, "shot through the forehead. As I knelt by the body and searched his pockets for the little trinkets that should be sent to his family and found there the pictures of the wife and the chubby children, and the locks of hair and soiled and worn letters from home, I felt like a murderer. The scene swam before my eyes and I fairly reeled. How I got through the rest of the day, God knows."

By around 2 p.m. there were other problems facing the 21st Ohio at Horseshoe Ridge as casualties had reduced their number to what was described as "a thin line of men." At this point in danger of being outflanked, they were saved by the timely arrival of General Steedman and his troops. As the afternoon wore on the constant firing of the repeating rifles caused them to overheat, preventing the gun's cylinders from revolving. The problems with the rifles gradually became a moot issue as the ammunition began to run low despite scrounging from the dead and wounded.

By around 4:30 p.m. ammunition was running low amongst the other regiments as well and General Thomas ordered a withdrawal and silence gradually replaced the sounds of gunfire. As a 6 p.m. sunset approached, most of the firing had stopped and smoke had wrapped the area in a ghostly fog blinding the troops on both sides. At around 6:30 the out-of-ammunition 21st Ohio, instead of being allowed to withdraw, was instead ordered to make a bayonet charge through the twilight, "an utterly useless movement," in the opinion of Lieutenant Vance.

Around 7 p.m. after several fruitless charges "with not even a shot to fire" the exhausted men of the regiment rested on a hill, now one of only three Union regiments left on the ridge as the rest had withdrawn. They saw a long line of soldiers advancing toward them through the shadows. "Wrapped in the fog they looked like so many phantoms on a ghostly brigade drill and it gave one a creepy sensation to look at them," Lieutenant Vance wrote.

Unsure if they were Union or Confederate, a captain went to investigate and was taken prisoner. Then a sergeant from Putnam County volunteered to go, a request to which Lieutenant Vance reluctantly agreed. The sergeant did not return either and Lieutenant Vance never saw him again. The rest of the regiment soon had their answer as with a yell and a volley of bullets, Confederate soldiers swarmed over them.

Some managed to flee in the darkness and confusion, including Lieutenant Vance. Running for his life, "the bullets were hunting me. I could hear them zip, zip, zipping all around and striking the earth and twigs all about me...Would I never get out of range? Those long-legged, lean fellows who were chasing me with the most abominable and offensive whooping and howling and shrill yelling seemed to keep right at my heels..." He made it to a Union position feeling "chagrined, forlorned and ashamed" for fleeing but soon was part of a larger retreat north toward Chattanooga.

The following day the remnants of the regiment assembled near Missionary Ridge in Chattanooga. "We were a sorry sight," wrote Lieutenant Vance. "No colors, no field officers, hungry, dirty and shabby." Then the general in command of their division rode up and demanded to know what regiment it was. When he was told he replied "My God! The 21st Ohio! It cannot be possible!"

"He seemed utterly overcome at the sight of the wreck of what the day before was his finest regiment" and tears ran down his face, wrote Lieutenant Vance. And the regiment was a wreck with 48 dead, over 100 wounded and around 120 taken prisoner for a casualty rate of nearly 50%. Of those taken prisoner, over 50 would die in Confederate prisons.

But the regiment's service had not been in vain as a frustrated Confederate General James Longstreet wrote of the battle, "Like magic, the Union army had melted away in our presence." And the 21st Ohio had played an important role in that melting away. It had held its position over six hours under intense enemy attack while firing over 43,000 rounds of ammunition. The regiment displayed "spectacular fighting with its Colt revolving rifles," in the words of historian Glenn Tucker, and "demonstrated that a regiment with efficient small arms could hold off two or three times their number." One lucky private in the regiment counted 23 holes shot through his clothing while his body received nary a scratch.

Horseshoe Ridge today is a place of quiet beauty that belies the violence that seared its hillsides on September 20, 1863. Part of the Chickamauga and Chattanooga National Military Park, the many markers there include a stone monument that honors the efforts of the 21st Ohio on that long and bloody day.

When the Civil War came to an end nearly two years later the 21st Ohio had one of the highest regimental ratios in the state of Ohio of men killed in battle or died of wounds. And with a total of nearly 400 deaths from all causes, the northwestern Ohio regiment had the dubious honor of ranking first of the state's approximately 250 infantry regiments and other military units, testament to their service and suffering.

General Steedman at Chickamauga

It was late in the morning on September 20th and the fighting along Horseshoe Ridge and Snodgrass Hill was intense as the bulk of the Union army continued in retreat. Absent from battle up to this point was General James B. Steedman, a division commander in the Reserve Corp, which consisted of three brigades that had been assigned a rear guard duty several miles north of the action. But as General Steedman and his superior at the scene, General Gordon Granger, peered through their binoculars to the south, it was obvious by the thunderous fire and the amount of smoke and dust rising in the air that Union forces there were in a great fight.

But General Granger's orders were somewhat unclear regarding maintaining his position or moving forward if events dictated and to violate orders, especially under battle conditions, could lead to court-martial and disgrace.

After a period of hesitation that left both generals anxious and champing at the bit, General Granger decided to go. He left one brigade behind and headed south with Steedman and two brigades toward the fighting. Smoldering woods, fields and houses along the way, Confederate sniper fire, and large numbers of dead and wounded foretold what was in store.

They arrived in the area around 1:30 during a brief lull in the fighting and their appearance on the scene with around 3,900 fresh soldiers and ammunition wagons hauling 95,000 rounds gave tremendous emotional lift to General Thomas and his forces. While the generals were discussing the next move the renewed sounds of heavy gunfire told them that Horseshoe Ridge had come under intense attack and General Thomas directed Steedman to take his two brigades and storm the ridge to the right of the 21st Ohio which by now was barely clinging to its position.

This plaque acknowledges the fighting of General Steedman and his troops on the afternoon of the second day of the battle of Chickamauga. It stands on Horseshoe Ridge in the Chickamauga and Chattanooga National Military Park.

General Steedman, after pausing to tell an aide to see that his name, frequently misspelled as Steadman, was spelled correctly in his obituary, moved to the fore and soon had his troops in position. About 2:15 bugles blared the call to fix bayonets and charge, the general raised up in his saddle and waved his hat, and with a loud cheer the Union line surged forward toward Horseshoe Ridge.

The ridge exploded in gunfire, so heavy at times it created a wall of sound where individual muskets could not be discerned. The hail of bullets shredded the trees, raining down leaves, bark, and twigs. The Union troops hurled themselves up the ridge and against the Confederate lines and for several minutes fought savagely at close quarters with bayonets, rifle butts, pistols and rocks. Union General John Palmer, observing through binoculars wrote, "In all my experience I have never witnessed such desperate hand-to-hand fighting."

General Steedman rode along the line encouraging the troops, at one point riding into a body of Illinois soldiers in retreat. Exhausted, frightened, and having suffered heavy losses, their colonel explained to the irritated general that he thought he could not get his troops to go back. His irritation quickly turned to anger. He told the colonel he was free to leave the field in disgrace, grabbed the regimental flag, and bellowed, "Go back if you like boys but the colors can't go with you" and charged up the ridge. The men turned around and followed.

Reaching the crest of the ridge General Steedman's horse was shot out from under him, flinging his burly figure to the ground and leaving him momentarily stunned and injuring his hands. He recovered, bound his bleeding hands and remained along the ridge, shouting and encouraging the troops. Horseshoe Ridge had been seized in only 20 minutes but casualties were horrific; nearly 20% of the general's soldiers were killed or wounded in that time and bodies lay everywhere. He would later describe the area as "a lake of blood."

For the next couple of hours the two sides charged and countercharged. Meanwhile the Union retreat went on and precious number of soldiers and armaments continued northward to safety as the soldiers of Horseshoe Ridge held their ground. Around 4:30 the shadows began to lengthen and the Union forces, running low on ammunition began a gradual withdrawal and the battle wound down. As the sun set around 6 p.m., Steedman and his surviving troops, out of ammunition, left the field and retreated toward the village of Rossville on the road to Chattanooga. As dusk became darkness around 7 p.m., an eerie quiet had settled over Horseshoe Ridge.

The defensive stand on Horseshoe Ridge turned what could have been a shattering Union defeat into a manageable one. The stand surely would have collapsed without the timely arrival and fighting of General Steedman and his brigades. As historian Francis McKinney put it, "this storming of [Horseshoe] Ridge by Steedman's men was the most spectacular and profitable counterattack of the day from the Union point of view. It accomplished in twenty minutes what (Confederate General) Longstreet tried for six hours to do."

The Union army retreated safely to Chattanooga to lick its wounds as Confederate General Braxton Bragg refused to pursue it, a decision for which he was bitterly criticized and which led to a premature end to his military career. The Confederates occupied the heights around the city and hunger and deprivation followed for the Union soldiers until General Ulysses Grant was able to break through with supplies and fresh troops. On November 23-25 Union forces, many of which were able to escape the field at Chickamauga, stormed the heights around Chattanooga in the battle of the same name. Confederate forces were routed and the way to Atlanta, the heart of the Confederacy, was laid open.

CHAPTER IV

JOHNSON'S ISLAND STORIES

The Prison

On the evening of April 11, 1862 a special train of the Sandusky, Dayton, and Cincinnati Railroad pulled into downtown Sandusky, Ohio. Two hundred men were hurriedly ushered from the train to a waiting steamer as local residents looked on with a mixture of curiosity and contempt. The men were not travelers or tourists but soldiers of the army of the Confederate States of America, now prisoners of war. Their destination was Johnson's Island in Sandusky Bay, named for its owner Leonard Johnson, where a newly built federal prison awaited its first arrivals.

The site had been selected the previous year after the secretary of war issued orders for an island prison on Lake Erie. It was believed at the time that the war would be a short one and the prison would be adequate to house all Confederate POW's taken, an estimate that would turn out to be woefully miscalculated. The Bass Islands and Kelley's Island had been also been considered but Johnson's Island was chosen for several reasons.

Its nearness to Sandusky made it easy to obtain supplies and lumber for building and eliminated the need for extensive storehouses; its limestone bed would discourage the digging of escape tunnels; in the event of a prisoner uprising or escape, the city of Sandusky could be notified via cannon shot to be ready to assist; the Sandusky shore to the south and the Marblehead Peninsula shore just to the north would discourage lake-borne rescue attempts by a rebel ship; and Johnson's Island, unlike Kelley's Island, had no winery to tempt the Union soldiers guarding the prison. The prison on Johnson's Island eventually came to be for Confederate officers only. And as officers tended to be better educated they left behind more of written record than might normally be expected. Over 12,000 prisoners of war would pass through the prison gates by war's

View during the war of the Confederate Prison on Johnson's Island as seen from Sandusky Bay. (From the Archives of Sandusky Library-Follet House Museum).

By the time the prison was in full operation at the end of 1863, it covered 15 acres with around 100 structures on the south side of the island facing the city of Sandusky. The prisoners slept in about a dozen two-story barracks, ranging in capacity from 150 to 270. The population of the prison fluctuated constantly due to paroles and prisoner exchanges between the North and the South. For example at the end of May, 1863 there were only 40 prisoners on hand. However when the exchanges were later halted the number swelled to over 3,200 at the end of 1864. The average prisoner count was in the 2,500 range.

The prison became an object of curiosity for area residents. Lake steamers, their decks lined with gazing passengers, would cruise slowly by much to the irritation of the prisoners. A Confederate lieutenant colonel described one such cruise in 1862: "We are brought here to be gazed at by a vulgar rabble as if we were caged hyenas. They would even stir us with a pole, if they dared, to see us growl (perhaps bite). What a commentary on frail humanity, showing the utter depravity of the human heart, the entire surrender of all that is manly and generous in the soul, to gratify a mere, idle curiosity. Woman, she whose mission is one of love and mercy, also throws her influence into the scale and jeers at the distressed. They are certainly not Christians..."

One of the consequences of life in any prison is boredom and despondency and the unwilling residents of Johnson's Island were no exception. To combat these they taught each other foreign languages, squared off in debate teams, and formed a theatrical group called "The Rebel Thespians" with admissions to shows 25 cents, 50 cents for a reserved seat. They also developed a circulating library that grew to over 500 books.

Some prisoners made and sold baked goods, furniture, jewelry and color drawings. Others profited by operating laundries that washed and ironed the clothes of their fellow inmates. One prisoner, Major George McNight from New Orleans, became well known for his talent as a poet writing under the *nom de plume* Asa Hartz (Ace of Hearts). Some of his poems were reprinted in area newspapers as well as a New York City paper. His lament "And No One Writes to Me" went in part:

The list is called and one by one
The anxious crowd now melts away
I linger and wonder why
No letter comes for me today.
Are all my friends in "Dixie" dead?

Or would they all forgotten be?
What have I done, what have I said
That no one writes to me?

When the poem was published, it had its desired effect as the author received nearly 60 letters and a dozen gift boxes from sympathizers.

The prisoners engaged in physical pursuits as well. Two baseball teams, one led by junior and the other by senior officers, were formed and played spirited games. In August, 1864 the "big game" between the two teams drew a crowd of 3,000 prisoners, guards, and Sandusky residents with no lack of wagering going on. Earlier that same year they divided up and engaged in a three-day "snowball war."

When it to came to diet, prison fare in 1862 and 1863 wasn't too bad as the Southerners enjoyed approximately the same rations as the Union soldiers guarding them. Additional food and goods could be purchased at the sutler store and from other local vendors allowed to sell to the prisoners and gifts and money could be received from home. In the summer of 1863 one prisoner wrote the Confederate secretary of war of the "kind and humane" treatment he was receiving.

But things changed when reports reached the North of the inhumane treatment of Union prisoners in the South, in particular at the prison at Andersonville, Georgia. By the summer of 1864 rations had been cut and provisions by way of purchase or gift had been banned or restricted and the gnawing ache of hunger became a daily companion for the inmates of Johnson's Island. The island's rat population began to dwindle as prisoners began catching and eating them. One group called themselves the "Rat Club" and, assisted by a terrier named Nellie, caught and sold rats for 10 cents apiece.

As in any prison at the time, disease and death were part of life on Johnson's Island. The limitations of mid-nineteenth century medical knowledge and treatment were aggravated by the island's limestone bed which prevented the digging of proper wells and latrines. Consequently the drinking water was often contaminated, leading to chronic diarrhea and dysentery. Diseases such as typhoid fever and pneumonia took their toll as well. However the overall death rate at the prison was only 2%, which was well below that of most other facilities. In February, 1865 for example, despite it being the middle of winter, only 2 deaths occurred out of a prison population of over 2,400.

The original grave markers in the Johnson's Island Confederate prison cemetery were made of wood. They were replaced with marble gravestones in 1890. (From the Archives of Sandusky Library- Follet House Museum).

On April 9, 1865 Robert E. Lee surrendered at Appomattox Court House and the Civil War came to an end. By June the details of release and transportation had been worked out and over 2,000 homesick Confederates passed through the prison gates for the last time. By the end of summer all the prisoners were gone and the prison was closed and Johnson's Island returned to being a peaceful Lake Erie atoll.

By the 1880's little evidence remained of the prison. Most of the prison buildings were gone and an orchard grew where prisoners barracks once stood. The prison cemetery had fallen into a state of neglect, its wooden headboards rotting away. In 1890 through the efforts of a group from Georgia the boards were replaced by white, marble stones, 206 in all. Fifty-four of the gravestones read simply, "Unknown."

In 1910 through the work of a Cincinnati chapter of the United Daughters of the Confederacy a bronze statue of a Confederate soldier was placed and dedicated to ensure "our unreturning brave have not been forgotten." The statue gazes out over Sandusky Bay, rifle in hand, standing permanent guard over the cemetery.

Confederate Pirates on Lake Erie

As the Civil War dragged on, the Confederacy experienced an increasing manpower shortage. Veteran officers were in particularly short supply and whiling away on Johnson's Island were enough of them to command 80,000 men. This led to a desperate plot to attack the island and free the officers imprisoned there.

Guarding the waters around Johnson's Island was the Navy gunboat, the *USS Michigan*, and the Confederates made plans to seize the ship and use it in their attack on the prison. Part of the plan involved bribing officers on the *Michigan* to go along with the scheme.

In August, 1864 a Confederate captain named Charles Cole moved into The West House, Sandusky's premier hotel at the time, posing as a wealthy, Pennsylvania oil man. There he flashed a lot of money and made acquaintance with many of the officers of the Michigan who frequented the hotel tavern. He wined and dined them, learning as much as he could about the ship, hoping to ultimately buy their participation. Meanwhile across Lake Erie in southern Ontario a group of Confederates was gathering and making plans as well. Their goal was to take control of one of the passenger steamers that regularly plied Lake Erie and sail to Sandusky Bay and the Michigan where hopefully, an on-board Charles Cole would signal them it was safe to seize the ship. It was a plan where too many things could go wrong.

On the morning of September 19th the passenger steamer *Philo Parsons* left Detroit on its usual run across the Detroit River to Ontario ports, then on to the Lake Erie islands and Sandusky city. About 30 men dressed as workers boarded in Ontario, men who were actually well-armed Confederate soldiers and agents under the leadership of Captain John Beall.

After the *Philo Parsons* had made its island stops and was steaming toward Sandusky Bay, the rebels sprang into action. There was some initial resistance on the part of the crew but a few gunshots convinced them otherwise and the ship was seized, a rare case of Great Lakes piracy. The crew and the thoroughly frightened passengers were herded below decks.

The *Philo Parsons* sailed toward Sandusky Bay where the Michigan would be visible and now things began to go wrong. The conspirators learned from the ship's engineer that there was little wood for fuel on board, that it normally refueled at Middle Bass Island after its Sandusky stop. The ship was ordered to be turned around and steam for Middle Bass. Its arrival there at an unscheduled time raised a bit of suspicion.

Now things got more complicated as a ship's whistle announced the approach of another passenger steamer, the *Island Queen*, making her regular stop. She pulled alongside and some of the rebels leaped to her deck and seized the ship, passengers and crew, the engineer receiving a gunshot wound to the face in the process. Included in the group were around 25 unarmed members of the 130th Ohio Volunteer Infantry enjoying a few vacation days before their scheduled mustering from service. Ironically after surviving their service they were POW's on their home turf.

Now the rebels had two ships and two boatloads of passengers and crew to deal with. They put the passengers and most of the crew onshore at Middle Bass, keeping a few crewmen to sail the *Philo Parsons*. They then towed the *Island Queen* about five miles out into the lake and scuttled her and headed again for Sandusky Bay and the Michigan. It was now well past sunset. Upon arriving at the entrance to the bay opposite the Marblehead Lighthouse the Confederates were informed by the crew that it was dangerous to enter the bay at night and that the Philo Parsons could easily run aground.

At this point the majority of the Confederates got cold feet and, in effect, mutinied. They turned the ship back toward Canada despite the objections of their leader Captain Beall. They wrote in a letter of protest to him that they believed their raid had been discovered and the enemy "is so well prepared that we can not by any possibility make it a success and, having already captured two boats, we respectfully decline to prosecute it further."

Their decision to turn back was a wise one as it turned out. Their man on the inside, Charles Cole, was in fact aboard the *Michigan*. But instead of being on deck ready to direct an attack on the ship he was below decks and in the brig. He had been arrested after a Confederate informer in Canada had alerted American authorities in Detroit of the plot. The *Michigan* and its crew were ready for an attack and had the rebel pirates aboard the *Philo Parsons* tried, they could have easily ended up at the bottom of Sandusky Bay.

Instead they sailed for Canadian waters. There they hoisted the Confederate flag on the ship, believed to be the only time that flag flew on Lake Erie during the war. They reached Canada early on the morning of September 20th, unloaded the crew on a Detroit River island, and docked at Sandwich, Ontario where they plundered and scuttled the *Parsons* before disappearing into the countryside. The Michigan sailed upriver in pursuit later that morning but it was too late.

The major consequence of the plot was the installation of additional cannon at Johnson's Island to guard against future attempts and the removal of the Confederate generals imprisoned there to another location for safer keeping. In addition the event gave the residents of Sandusky and the Lake Erie Islands something to talk about for a time.

Both the scuttled *Island Queen* and *Philo Parsons* were easily refloated and repaired and back on their passenger runs within a week. Captain Beall continued his anti-Union activities along the U.S.-Canadian border and was caught, court-martialed, and hung in February, 1865. Charles Cole was sent to prison and released in 1866. While he claimed he had successfully bribed both crew members of the *Michigan* and Union personnel at Johnson's Island to assist in the aborted Confederate raid, no evidence ever surfaced to substantiate his claim.

The Escape Artist

Charles Pierce was a lieutenant from Louisiana, a popular man who played on the prison baseball team and was involved in their theatrical productions. The lieutenant also had another passion: escaping.

His first recorded attempt came when he organized a digging party to tunnel under the fence. The tunnel was completed but when the diggers came through it they emerged at the feet of a waiting guard. On another occasion a garbage cart was driven into the prison yard one morning by a soldier who'd had a bit to drink for breakfast. While the cart was being filled the soldier laid down in Pierce's block for a nap. While he was sleeping, Pierce relieved him of his cap and overcoat and drove the cart past the guards and out the prison gate. However the sleeping soldier was soon discovered and Pierce was caught and returned to the prison.

Another attempt was made by constructing crude ladders from scrap material and, on a moonlit night, scaling the prison wall with two others. One was shot and one was caught right away but Pierce made to the Marblehead Peninsula. However some farmers there, alerted by the gunfire, were waiting and captured him, receiving the usual reward money of $100.

Pierce, now under close observation, would make one more attempt. He managed to procure a Union uniform and spent five months constructing a rifle out of wood and metal from discarded cans, which looked remarkably like the real thing. On the given day he started a rumor that there would be an escape attempt that night and waited for an inspection party of guards that would be sure to come and investigate.

When they came, he fell into ranks with them in his uniform and shouldering his facsimile gun. But the beauty of things lies in the details sometimes and Pierce had overlooked one: he had forgotten to make a cartridge box, which would have been easy to make. When the guard was lined up for inspection, the officer in charge noticed Pierce's lack of a cartridge box then demanded to inspect his rifle and his ruse came to an end. He would make no more attempts after that and was paroled at the end of the war with the rest of the prisoners.

The Ohio Rebel

Of all the Confederate prisoners imprisoned on Johnson's Island one of the more unusual ones was Edmund DeWitt Patterson. What made him different was his heritage; that of an Ohio boy born and raised in adjacent Lorain County. The educated and articulate Patterson also kept a journal through the course of the war, including his time on Johnson's Island.

Patterson grew up on a Lorain County farm and, in 1859 at the age of 17, decided to seek his fortune as a traveling salesman of books and magazines. Three months of this convinced him the salesman's life was not for him and he quit. Now in Alabama, he was reluctant to return home fearing he would be laughed at over his poor career choice and instead found work as a teacher.

As the Civil War drew nearer, tensions began to rise and Northerners living in the South were looked upon with suspicion and Patterson decided to return to Ohio. But when someone accused him of being a spy, he decided to remain, apparently to prove his accuser wrong. When the war broke out, he embraced the cause of the Confederacy and in May, 1861 joined an Alabama infantry unit.

He saw his first combat a year later at the Battle of Williamsburg, Virginia, and was seriously wounded, shot in the shoulder and in both legs. He went on to survive a grueling, nearly four-month recovery. After a furlough back to Alabama he rejoined the Confederate army in November, now a lieutenant. He would serve until July 2, 1863 when taken prisoner at the Battle of Gettysburg. After a brief stay at Fort Delaware, he was transferred to Johnson's Island, arriving there July 20th.

Patterson found his surroundings on Johnson's Island to be a major improvement compared to Fort Delaware which has been described as a "hellhole." His father, sister and uncle came to visit at the end of the month but were not allowed face-to-face contact.

On August 18th his father visited and was allowed to see him, and urged his son to take the oath of loyalty to the Union, which would enable his release. Patterson was adamant in his refusal and it's obvious by the tone of his writings that day he had embraced the Confederate cause, heart, mind and soul. "I can scarcely consider myself a member of the family," he wrote, "we have nothing in common."

In September he wrote of having episodes of despondency fueled substantially by inner conflict between loyalty to the South and loyalty to family. "Here I am near the spot where I passed the sunny hours of childhood and the golden dreaming days of youth and under what circumstances—a prisoner of war. I am devoted to a cause that I esteem a just and holy one, and here is a kind father who I believe loves me as he loves his own life—two sisters whose love for me is as pure as an Angel's love, and my brothers too—yet all regard me as forever disgraced and dishonored."

As the year wore on Patterson wrote of daily life in prison: of illnesses, of shortages of firewood, of the weather, etc. But he wrote also of the intellectual and recreational pursuits the prisoners were allowed to engage in. Glancing about his barracks at the end of October and seeing one prisoner studying French, another reading a novel, others playing chess while still others were writing letters or playing cards he observed, "If a stranger were to look in on us this morning he would hardly think we were prisoners." As the year 1863 came to an end he made a lengthy entry on New Years Eve expounding on the nobility of the Southern cause and expressing confidence it would somehow prevail.

During the winter he wrote little until February 22nd, George Washington's birthday, which both sides celebrated. Calling the Yankee celebration of the day a "mockery," he wrote, "they celebrate the birthday of a Southern gentleman and a slaveholder, and this while they are straining every nerve to tear down what he built up..."

On March 20th Patterson observed his 22nd birthday, but with no joy. "Twenty-two years gone and how little I have accomplished! It is with a feeling of sadness that I view the scene which memory too faithfully spreads before me. When I realize what I am and contrast it with what I might have been, I pronounce my life a failure."

As the weather warmed, so did Patterson's pen as his entries started to become more numerous. Many entries in May refer to reports and rumors of battles in Virginia which he followed with intense interest. The Union had begun a major campaign against Robert E. Lee's Army of Northern Virginia and casualties were enormous. On May 14th he wrote, "this state of suspense and nervous excitement is wearing me down." The next day, despairing at the loss of life on both sides, he penned, "Madness rules the hour. Why this terrible sacrifice of human life?...Will they rebaptize Virginia in blood? What a sight for the world, what a scene for God and the angels to look upon."

In June Patterson reflected on the lack of privacy of prison life. "Perhaps one of the worst features of prison life at this place at present is that it is so public, that is it is impossible to get away from the crowd, the bustle, and confusion....there is not a spot within the walls of this prison to which one can go for quiet reflection and meditation."

On July 2nd, the one-year anniversary of his capture at Gettysburg, Patterson was in a dark mood. "I am almost ready to say let this day be stricken from the calendar...little did I think at that time that long weary months would elapse ere I would again join the company of my brave boys." And on July 20th, the anniversary of his arrival on Johnson's Island, he wrote, "It is so hard to be shut up here when our country needs us so much. It would be better, it seems to me, to be killed at once on the battlefield."

On August 7th he wrote of a friend who had died with whom he had spent considerable time in his final days. "My friend, Lt. McRae died. I hope he is better off now. He suffered much during the last few days of his life, but without a murmur. One by one they are passing away. God grant that I may live to return South! I do not wish to die on this lonely island."

On August 25th he received a letter from a cousin named Angie informing him that she had nothing to say to him, that there was no place in her heart for a cousin who had taken the Confederate cause. On the 30th Patterson's father and brother came to the island. They were allowed to view each other from a distance but not speak.

Mid-September found Patterson losing weight, along with the rest of the prisoners, as rations had been cut. Prisoners were now eating rats, something Patterson wanted nothing to do with. A friend, however, had made a large, rat stew and Patterson relented. "They taste very much like a young squirrel and would be good enough if called by any other name," he wrote.

On the evening of September 24th the prison was struck by a severe thunderstorm with high winds and possibly a tornado. As his barracks building began to rock he leaped from his bed to flee when the roof was ripped off. He ended up outside and was blown along the ground and, by the flash of lightning, could see other men being tossed about as well. In the aftermath he was surprised to find he had only minor bumps and bruises. The experience, of course, was terrifying. "I think I would prefer fighting a battle every morning before breakfast rather than experience a repetition of last night's work," he wrote.

The windstorm left a number of prison buildings damaged and large quantities of lumber were brought in for repairs. This led to a cat and mouse game between the guards and prisoners as the latter sought to pilfer the lumber. They needed the wood to make repairs to their bunks and for other improvements as parts of the wooden infrastructure of the barracks had been used as firewood the previous winter. The prisoners created a number of diversions to distract the guards and soon had acquired a substantial amount of lumber that they hid under the barracks for later use. "I think if we had a few more tools we could build a gunboat," Patterson wrote.

In October, the short rations and hunger continued. "I go to bed and get up hungry, and go hungry through the day and at night dream of something to eat. Men go about looking so cadaverous, with their sunken cheeks and thin, blue lips that it is fearful to look at them."

The portion of Patterson's diary from October 6, 1864 to March 14, 1865 is missing. On the latter date, "a blessed day in the calendar," Patterson was released along with 300 other prisoners. He made his way to Virginia where he caught up with his old regiment. "Oh how much has changed since I last saw them. I miss so many faces that used to greet me. A mere handful remains of the little band; they have been wasted by the storms of battle and disease and even the few remaining look weary and worn."

On April 9th his last diary entry concluded with, " I fear there is terrible fighting in store for us this summer but the Almighty may care for us as He has in the past." However this would not be as Robert E. Lee surrendered to Ulysses Grant at Appomattox Court House that same day. And for Edmund DeWitt Patterson and countless others, the Civil War and its sorrow and suffering came to an end.

From *Yankee Rebel: The Civil War Journal of Edmund DeWitt Patterson*, edited by John G. Barrett. Copyright (c) 1966 by the University of North Carolina Press. Used by permission of the publisher

The Deserter

Of the thousands of prisoners to pass through the gates of Johnson's Island, there were a few from the Union side, one of whom was named Reuben Stout. Stout was originally from Pennsylvania and moved to Indiana in his early twenties. In December, 1861 he enlisted in an Indiana infantry regiment. In 1862 his regiment was captured in Kentucky and sent home in November to Indiana as part of a prisoner exchange. There the men received a few days furlough.

While on furlough Stout became ill and was laid up for a couple of weeks. It was during this time he began receiving, and heeding, bad advice. He was told by various others not to return, that it was an "abolition war," and that The Knights of the Golden Circle, a Northern group sympathetic to the Confederacy, would protect him if he joined. The goals of the group were to resist not only the emancipation of slaves but the war itself in any way possible. He attended a secret meeting of the group and took their oath. Reuben Stout was now a deserter.

After about four months of hiding out at the home of his father-in-law, he went to stay with his brother near Delphi, Ind. and on the second night two men came to arrest him. Stout, who was hiding upstairs, later claimed he overheard one of the men saying he was going to shoot him. As that man ascended the stairs, Stout opened fire, killing him.

He fled but was pursued by a posse and caught and arrested

the next day. Charged now with both murder and desertion, there would be no mercy. At his court martial in May, 1863, he was sentenced to "be shot to death with musketry" the following October and sent to the prison at Johnson's Island. There, as his final hours wound down, he wrote down his thoughts.

The Johnson's Island Confederate prison cemetery as seen today.

"I was led by evil counsels, and my connection with a secret, traitorous organization, to stay away from my post of duty in the army. I am truly sorry that I acted thus, or that I for a moment listened to those evil counsels. I am sorry that I ever lifted my hand against the life of my fellow man. I think the man who came to arrest me did not act right, but I do not excuse myself for my wrongdoing on that account. I would affectionately and earnestly urge all in the service of their country not to do as I have done but to be faithful to their obligations as soldiers..."

"I have sought mercy at the hand of God. I die trusting in the Lord and Savior Jesus Christ. I believe God is gracious and therefore enjoy peace in this sad and solemn hour. I bear no malice to my enemies or accusers. I hope my death may do good as a warning to others. Commending my dear wife— with our four children— to the kind keeping of a merciful Providence, I take my leave of this world, hoping to meet them in a world where sorrow and death will never come."

On October 23, 1863, a day described as "cold, dark, and cheerless" by the Ohio rebel Edmund DeWitt Patterson, a heavily chained and thoroughly frightened Reuben Stout was led out to the beach on the south shore of the island where a firing squad was arranged in an open square. There a Sandusky minister met with him and they talked and prayed together. He was then seated on the edge of his coffin and a hood was lowered over his head. An absolute stillness fell over the scene and "the suspense became painful in the extreme," according Patterson. "His crime was forgotten and we saw only a fellow human being trembling on the verge of another world."

The firing squad then leveled their rifles and took aim. The command was given. And the roar of gunfire echoed over the still waters of Sandusky Bay as the life of Reuben Stout came to an end.

Ghosts of the Confederacy

History is full of stories that fall well within the realm of the speculative and perhaps none so much as the story of what some quarry workers experienced one terrifying night on Johnson's Island. In the early part of the 1900's, well after the island's prison days had passed, a group of Italian quarry workers lived in a clutch of rough shacks while working the limestone quarry on the island.

Late one winter a furious March storm raged over the island and Sandusky Bay making any escape back to the mainland out of the question. So strong was the wind that the workers feared their shacks would be blown away and sought refuge among the trees and the statue of the soldier at the Confederate cemetery. The men lay low as the wind howled and the waves slammed against the island shore.

As they huddled shivering they heard the sound of bugles. They looked up at the statue of the Confederate soldier and to their astonishment it turned slowly toward the marble grave-stones of the cemetery. Astonishment turned to terror as one-by-one hollow-eyed men in gray uniforms rose from their graves, muskets on shoulder. The ghostly army formed silently in ranks before marching through the cemetery and toward the south, disappearing into the black Lake Erie night.

The workers fled back to their shacks and remained there until the storm abated. As soon as safely possible they hurried to the mainland, pouring out their story to anyone who would listen. What really happened that stormy March night may never be known. It was said, however, that no amount of convincing could persuade any of the quarry workers to ever return to Johnson's Island.

Note: While Johnson's Island is privately owned, the cemetery with informational displays and parking area are open to the public.

This statue of a Confederate soldier has been standing guard over the graves of his comrades on Johnson's Island since 1910.

CHAPTER V

THE 111TH OHIO VOLUNTEER INFANTRY

Note: The author of the history of the 111th Ohio Volunteer Infan-
try, Wesley S. Thurstin of Wood County, began the Civil War as a
first sergeant and was promoted to lieutenant then to captain at war's
end. At the initial regimental reunion in Perrysburg in 1878 he was
asked to compile a regimental history. Relying mostly on recollection
and reminiscences and not on official records, his effort was pub-
lished in 1894. His work was, in his words, "not designed along the
lines of historical severity in treatment of the subject matter but rather
in the lighter vein of enjoyable reminiscences of army life."

The 111th Ohio Volunteer Infantry represented a broad spec-
trum of northwestern Ohio. Of its ten companies Wood County
provided all of companies B and D and the greater parts of I
and K; companies A and G were principally from Sandusky
County; Company H hailed from Lucas County; while companies C, E and F were a blend of soldiers from Defiance,
Fulton, Williams, and Lucas counties. They were mustered into
service on the 5th and 6th of September, 1862 at Camp Toledo,
a collection of barracks north of the city's downtown area that
served as a base for organization and rudimentary training.

After a few days the regiment, around 1,050 strong, was
loaded onto freight cars of the Dayton and Michigan Railroad
and shipped out of Toledo. They arrived in Perrysburg after
dark where the women of the town greeted them with baskets
of food and bouquets of flowers and whose cheers filled their
ears as the train left. They received a similar welcome in Cin-

cinnati and crossed the Ohio River on a pontoon bridge on September 14th, many of them purchasing a poorly done wood-cut engraving of the crossing, soon realizing that the image could have been of any regimental crossing.

They continued south in a warm Kentucky autumn where the 111th Ohio received its first taste of the deprivations of an army on the march: "clouds of suffocating dust, the pitiless Southern sun, the intolerable thirst which drove us to fill our canteens at horse ponds polluted by dead or dying mules," according to Captain Thurstin.

They would go on to spend a long winter at Bowling Green, Kentucky. "Then came our winter camp life with nothing between us between the frost and snow except the sheet of canvas. Men were packed like sardines in a box, sleeping on the ground. Epidemics raged throughout the camp. The graveyard threatened to become more populous than the camp itself and when spring came over two hundred men out of the original one thousand had died or been discharged because of physical disability," wrote Captain Thurstin.

At the end of May, 1863 the 111th Ohio left Bowling Green and in July were steaming up the Ohio River taking part in the pursuit of Morgan's Raiders, capturing about 50 of them on an island. [Confederate General John Hunt Morgan led a force of around 2,500 cavalrymen on a daring, 1,000 mile-plus raid through parts of Tennessee, Kentucky, Indiana, and Ohio before surrendering about 25 miles south of Youngstown. The raid was the Confederacy's northernmost penetration of the war.] The regiment then spent some time in Cincinnati before returning to Kentucky.

During that summer the men became adept at the art of foraging for food and other necessities. At times they used bank bills from the Erie and Kalamazoo Railroad, Toledo's first railroad, which had gone bankrupt in the 1840's, as a medium of exchange, so to speak. "With Erie and Kalamazoo Railroad bank bills, all things were possible," wrote Captain Thurstin. "That was the great inflation period. If any Rebel presumed to doubt the legal tender qualities of that money he was laughed to scorn (and) was informed that his early financial education had been neglected, and as a punishment for his dense ignorance on the subject his property was taken without money and without price."

November found the regiment in Tennessee where it would see its first serious action in the Battle of Knoxville. By the middle of the month Confederate General James Longstreet had drawn near with an army of over 35,000 and the 111th Ohio found itself part of an all night, chaotic retreat to avoid being encircled. During this night over half of Company B from Wood County was captured. This was followed by furious fighting and a retreat to Knoxville where "we threw our knapsacks on the ground and, utterly exhausted, sank to sleep," Captain Thurstin wrote. "For three days and nights you had been on your feet; human endurance could stand no more fatigue." After a too short respite, the exhausted men began nearly three weeks of trench warfare as Longstreet's forces besieged the city. "The days wore on. The enemy's shot and shell were playing tennis in the streets. Famine threatened. Our horses, mules and cattle were dying from starvation and, as the carcasses floated down the Holston (River), were greeted with rebel cheers."

The Confederates ended their siege on December 6th and the 111th Ohio went on to spend a relatively peaceful winter camped along a picturesque stream called Mossy Creek. "Nature had surpassed itself in creating an ideal trout stream, from the channel of which the surface ground rose gently in grassy slopes, with groves of trees here and there forming altogether the most enjoyable and reposeful camp grounds we could have hoped for," noted Captain Thurstin.

Their restful winter and early spring ended in late April, 1864 when they went on the march again south, part of the Army of the Ohio under General William Tecumseh Sherman, and soon to take part in the Atlanta campaign. "Thence come the memories of mud, dead mules to windward, objects along the lines of march and countermarch seen so often in our marches and countermarches as to have become not only uninteresting but hateful to us," wrote the captain.

May 14th found the regiment lining up on a ridge of a creek valley preparing to charge a heavily fortified rebel ridge on the opposite side, an event that would be known as the Battle of Resaca. Inspecting the ridge in the morning Captain Thurstin rode to the commanding general's headquarters and requested that artillery be brought in before any such charge was made. His request was treated in an "indifferent manner" and, in fact, no such artillery support was sent.

Later in the day the order to charge was given and the result was a blood bath. As they charged through the valley the 111th Ohio and its fellow regiments were met with a storm of lead. The majority of them sought refuge in a creek where many of their guns became jammed with mud and water. They were ordered to return to the ridge and then to make a second fruitless charge before given the order to retreat.

"We had been made the victims of an inexcusable blunder," wrote Captain Thurstin. "Our regiment went into that action with over five hundred muskets and came out of it so crippled that were able to muster only 107 guns when we rallied on the ridge. The upturned faces down the hill side, in the valley, and the bodies floating in the muddy water of the creek accounted for some of them. The ambulances and stretcher bearers reported others." After dark Captain Thurstin and another officer crept down to the battlefield and could hear in the distance the muffled voices of rebel soldiers robbing the dead and wounded.

Resaca would be the first of a chain of battles in the Atlanta campaign and for the 111th Ohio it would be the costliest thus far with six killed or dying from wounds and ten wounded severely enough to be discharged from service. After Resaca the regiment continued to advance, on one day coming upon a large plantation. "Any one can readily imagine how grieved we were upon approaching the fine mansion house that the owner did not come out to meet us and insist we should make his home ours...we soon recovered from the surprise, however, and waiving the trifling informality of invitation, made ourselves at home." The owner had long since fled.

About 400 soldiers spent the night in the plantation house which was "superbly furnished," according to Captain Thurstin. "Pier glasses rested upon marble slabs; oil paintings adorned parlor walls; great bell glasses covered cunning works of art in wax, ebony and gold." The next morning they were back on the march and "for 72 days, without intermission, we were in the line of battle and every day under fire."

In early September the regiment was camped outside Atlanta when a tremendous flash lit the night sky with a following explosion that shook the ground beneath them. "We readily guessed the cause," noted Captain Thurstin. "We had cut the last artery of commerce which could sustain Atlanta's life and

Part of the staff of the 111th O.V.I which was mustered in Toledo. Seated in bottom row far right is Captain Wesley S. Thurstin who authored the history of the regiment. The others are, top row left to right, Lieutenants Isaac E. Kintigh, Louis Dienst, Gus F. Smith, Patrick F. Dalton, and Captain Henry J. McCord. Seated in bottom row left to right, Lieutenant Myron G. Brown, Captain Julius D. Bowles, Major John E. McGowan, and Captain Patrick H. Dowling. (Toledo-Lucas County Public Library.)

the rebel general [Hood], who had been called to 'drive the invaders from the sacred soil,' was then engaged in the very humiliating business of destroying his ordinance stores preparatory to evacuating the city."

By the time Atlanta fell the 111th Ohio was a thoroughly seasoned, and confident, regiment. "The experience of officers and soldiers alike, extending from the 5th of May to the 2nd day of September, or 120 days under fire, had accomplished more in the way of educating soldiers in the art of war than all the previous campaigns had done...We felt such confidence in ourselves, such certainty that no force which the rebels could collect could drive us out of our way...The men who ventured timidly into the woods of northern Georgia were now expressing a hope that 'Uncle Billy' (General Sherman) would take them through to the sea."

The 111th spent the autumn of 1864 in pursuit of General Hood and his Army of Tennessee, finally meeting in battle near Franklin, Tennessee on the last day of November, a brutal fight in which the confidence and experience of the regiment would be put to its most grueling test of the war. The Confederates made charge after hopeless charge, each time being mowed down by the murderous fire of Union troops. "Our men fired so rapidly that many of their guns became disabled," wrote Captain Thurstin. "The guns of dead and wounded were loaded by the officers and men in the rear rank and exchanged for empty guns with the men in front. Soon the cry 'Give us more ammunition' ran up and down the line...The tempest of lead and iron beat the surface of the earth into dust, as the spray upon great waters leaps under the lash of the advancing storm."

The regiment fought "bayonet to bayonet and muzzle to muzzle" as it never had before and when the smoke had cleared the Confederates had lost over 6,000 men including five generals in only a few hours time. A distraught Tennessee resident observed, "O my God! What did we see! It was a great holocaust of death...I was never so horrified and appalled in my life."

The 111th Ohio suffered 17 killed or mortally wounded and

a good number more seriously wounded, its worst one-day casualties of the war. "If the Moslem conceit be true that the gates of paradise stand open for those who worthily die in a good cause, the names all glow upon the muster roll of the Great Commander," a saddened Captain Thurstin noted. "Several of them I knew very intimately and the best tribute I can give them is but scant justice to their merit."

A war correspondent examining the Franklin battlefield in the aftermath wrote that he "never saw evidences of so terrible a conflict as can be seen in front of a line occupied by the One Hundred and Eleventh Ohio. I counted twelve locust trees in one cluster, the size of a man's thigh, that were literally shot off with musket balls. In a grove covering about one-half the regimental front I think there were not less than two hundred such trees shot down...The rebels buried their own dead where they fell. There are between ninety and one hundred rebel dead buried in front of the ground occupied by the One Hundred and Eleventh Ohio." And the *Nashville Daily Times* wrote of the 111th Ohio, "This fine regiment was exposed to the shock of the rebel charges at Franklin and sustained them with signal valor."

After the Battle of Franklin the 111th Ohio withdrew to Nashville and participated in the battle of the same name on December 15th and 16th in which the remnants of Hood's army were literally chased away. Of the second day of the battle Captain Thurstin wrote of his fellows, "Then came your turn to charge and through the adjacent corn field you went with a rush, and over the works pell mell without meeting even a show of resistance... Hood's army had gone like leaves before a whirl wind."

The 111th Ohio saw no more action in the area after Nashville and in midwinter was sent to North Carolina to join Union forces fighting there. The regiment made a generally miserable river and rail journey to Ohio then through Virginia to Washington D.C. where some of them met President Abraham Lincoln at a reception. After that they were loaded onto an old steamer, "such a cranky old hulk that her name does not deserve to be perpetuated, even in a regimental history," wrote

Captain Thurstin. They were advised by the mate to tie their possessions down lest they be thrown about in a storm. But the landlubbers from northwest Ohio declined as "we thought at the time it was a marine joke."

That night as they steamed along the coast a violent winter storm set in. Captain Thurstin, after being thrown under a table a couple of times, found himself clinging to his bunk for life as most of their tents and other equipment were "going overboard to the whales as fast as possible." They had taken the precaution of tying down their precious mess chest containing various foods and some fine china appropriated from a Georgia plantation but the ropes soon gave way and it was smashed. However the worst was yet to come when the coal stove in their cabin tore from the floor spilling hot coals which started two fires. They were now caught on the open sea in a raging storm on a ship that was on fire.

The frightened men of the 111th Ohio frantically fought the flames with their wool blankets until the crew of the lurching ship was able to bring water hoses to bear and douse the fires. When morning came the seas had calmed but most of the men were still in a state of semi-shock, mitigated at times by violent seasickness. The rest of the voyage proceeded without incident and soon they were ashore in North Carolina carrying "a wholesome dislike to anything marine," according to Captain Thurstin.

They spent a few days at Fort Fisher, a seaside Confederate fort that had recently fallen to Union forces following an intense naval bombardment. "The sand plain around and inside the fort was so nearly covered with shot and shell from the guns of the fleet that one could have easily walked over the field without touching the ground." After getting into trouble for an unauthorized appropriation of lumber to build shelters (all their tents lay at the bottom of the ocean) they were sent down the coast to make camp along the shore. There they roasted oysters on driftwood fires and "we would have been satisfied to stay as long as the 'good of the service' should have required," noted the captain.

They soon were on the march up the Cape Fear River to Wilmington, North Carolina which Confederate soldiers abandoned with only token resistance. They entered the city on February 22nd, Washington's birthday, and found the citizens there tired of war: "The old domineering, supercilious spirit manifested by the Southern people in the early years of the war was no longer exhibited."

They remained in Wilmington a couple of weeks doing garrison duty and aiding some Union prisoners of war who had been paroled. "Language is inadequate to describe their condition," Captain Thurstin wrote. "Starvation by slow degrees had rendered nearly all of them as helpless as children." In March they left Wilmington and marched toward the interior of the state, the road at times lined with former slaves greeting them with a "fantastic exhibition of joy...to them we were angels of deliverance from the bondage of enforced and unremunerated toil."

On April 11th the 111th Ohio was resting while on the march toward Raleigh when an officer came galloping down the road shouting and waving his hat. Robert E. Lee had surrendered and the war was over. "Through the sunshine of that April day there suddenly burst upon us that great American holiday, the Fourth of July," wrote Captain Thurstin. Guns were fired and homemade fireworks were fashioned in a celebration that lasted well into the night. "The news was not alone the news of victory to the Union arms. It was also the recognized tolling of bells for the death of the Confederacy. It meant a reunited country. The triumph of right. The humiliation of wrong."

The regiment remained in North Carolina until June 23rd when they were mustered out of service and ordered to Cleveland for final discharge. July 4th found them on a train steaming through Pennsylvania where citizens met them at the stations, showering them with food. "The fresh white bread and golden butter revived the memories of our mother's cupboards at home. We had seen and tasted nothing like it since midsummer, 1862." They reached Cleveland the next day, and, after several days of settling various matters, were ready to say goodbye and scatter to their northwest Ohio homes. Tears flowed and voices trembled and halted.

"Men who for nearly three years had stood side by side on

the battle field, who had saved each other from death or capture, who had nursed each other in sickness and who had preserved, unbroken, the tenderest life friendships in health were to separate, perhaps forever," Captain Thurstin wrote. "Pictures were taken and exchanged, the last farewells said, and the old regiment disappeared forever."

When the 111th Ohio left Toledo in September, 1862 it numbered around 1,050 men. When discharged from service in Cleveland nearly 3 years later it numbered only 432. Of the over 600 who did not finish the war with their regiment, around 400 were discharged for various reasons, primarily disability resulting from wounds or illness. The rest, 206, never returned to northwest Ohio, having died in battle, or of wounds, disease, accidents, or in Confederate prisons. The first to die was Private Martin Tracy of Company K on November 1, 1862. His cause of death was not given though probably of disease, and he was buried in Louisville, Kentucky. The last to die was Private Albert Anderson, also of Company K, who died June 19, 1865, again probably of disease, and was buried in Raleigh, North Carolina.

The other dead of the 111th Ohio were buried on battlefields and in cemeteries across the South, including two who were buried at Arlington National Cemetery who died in February, 1865 while the regiment was en route to North Carolina. And of the 206 who died, 28 unfortunate souls perished in Confederate prisons, all but two at the notorious lock-up at Andersonville, Georgia.

There can be little doubt that the 111th Ohio fought very admirably and, in the process, represented northwestern Ohio well. For on July 6, 1865 the *Cleveland Daily Herald* wrote simply, "There is no regiment that has a better fighting record than the 111th Ohio."

CHAPTER VI

Petroleum V. Nasby

"I'll publish, right or wrong: Fools are my theme, let satire be my song," once wrote the English poet Lord Byron. His words could easily have described Findlay publisher David Ross Locke whose satirical writings during the Civil War gave Northerners aid and comfort, from citizens on the home front to the Union soldier in the field to President Abraham Lincoln in the White House.

Locke wrote regular essays using the pen name of Petroleum V. Nasby called the Nasby Letters that lampooned Copperheads, or Northerners sympathetic to the Southern cause. Locke's Nasby character advanced their arguments, but in a manner that made them sound ridiculous. Copperheads were portrayed as red-necked and red-nosed, ignorant bumpkins and bigots blinded by partisanship and self-interest. The Nasby letters were crude by today's standards and employed ethnic and racial slurs, reflecting the norms of the time for humorous writing.

One of Locke's biggest fans was President Lincoln himself who enjoyed reading the Nasby letters aloud to White House visitors. He was also known to read them as a source of refuge when the stress of the office and the war were weighing heavily upon him. After the war George Boutwell, secretary of the treasury under President Ulysses Grant, said the Union's victory could be attributed to "the army, the navy, and the Nasby letters."

Born September 20, 1833 in the vicinity of Binghamton, New York, Locke's family roots ran deep into the history of the country as his grandfather had fought in the American Revolution and was said to have participated in the throwing of tea from British ships in Boston Harbor. Locke's early years were marked by tragedy as several siblings and his mother died when he was a child. But he did inherit from his father strong humanitarian convictions including a dim view of slavery.

An avid reader, by the age of 12 Locke was working as an apprentice printer. At the age of 17 he left home and spent the next few years wandering from town to town working for newspapers and learning as much about the business as he could. He ended up in Pittsburgh, working for a time for the *Pittsburgh Chronicle.* There he worked as a reporter and assistant editor and got his first taste of writing editorials. When a strike shut the paper down in 1853 Locke headed west to Ohio seeking to run his own newspaper.

He got his first opportunity in Plymouth, Ohio, not far from

The man who created Petroleum V. Nasby, David Ross Locke. (Toledo-Lucas County Public Library).

Mansfield. There he published the *Advertiser* where he first experimented in humorous writing that would lead to his Petroleum V. Nasby character. He sold the paper in 1855 and bought and briefly published a paper in Mansfield before moving on to Crawford County and Bucyrus, acquiring the *Journal* in the spring of 1856. This newspaper was the Republican organ in a county dominated by Democrats and Locke began embracing Republican positions and doing editorial battle with the Democratic paper in town—it was typical then for newspapers to be openly aligned with a political party.

In 1857 when the Supreme Court handed down its Dred Scott decision which denied Congress the power to ban slavery in the territories and denied blacks citizenship, Locke wrote, "The fact is, every department of government is now under the control of slave power. The Bench—the Judiciary has prostituted itself, and henceforth there is no hope but in the virtue of the people." Locke's anti-slavery views and his contempt for those who thought differently continued to harden.

In addition to strong editorials Locke continued to enjoy experimenting with different types of irreverent and humorous writing for the amusement of his readers. He was also began using creative spelling to communicate a crude, backwoods dialect in some of his writing, a style that would come to trademark his Nasby letters. In 1859 a verse titled "Sonnnit—Beer and the Inventur Tharof" appeared in the *Journal* that began:

> Beer, you'm good—refreshin tis 2 se
> The creamy fome kurl o'er the portly glass,
> Tis 'nuf 2 maik I wish the likwid pas
> Size was as long as an orthodox eternity
> Good!—you'm better as good! We I hev kwaft
> 15 or 16 glasses, mi sad sole
> Rises ore erth, and finds its sawt for gole
> There's dubble-bariled exstasy in the draft!

As the decade wound down and national events were sweeping the country toward civil war, Locke became a staunch supporter of Abraham Lincoln and had personal interviews with him on a couple of occasions. Upon Lincoln's November, 1860 election a headline in the *Bucyrus Journal* exclaimed, "The Most Glorious Triumph Ever Achieved!"

In December, as South Carolina moved to secede from the Union, Locke mocked that state via a satirical editorial calling for Crawford County to secede from Ohio that went in part:

Our whole history has been one of aggression on the part of the State.

It refused to locate the Capitol at Bucyrus, to the great detriment of our real estate owners.

It refused to gravel the streets of Bucyrus or even re-lay the plank road.

It refused to locate the Penitentiary at Bucyrus, notwithstanding we do as much towards filling it as any other county.

It refused to locate the State Fair at Bucyrus, thus blighting the hopes of our free, independent and patriotic pea-nut vendors.

It has compelled us, year after year, to pay our share of the state taxes.

It put us in the same Congressional district with Ottawa county.

No citizen of this county has ever been appointed to any place where theft is possible.

When war broke out months later, Locke was appalled that there were people in Crawford County who continued to remain sympathetic toward the South and railed against them editorially, referring to them as "Masked Traitors."

In November, 1861 David Ross Locke left Bucyrus for Hancock County and Findlay where he took control of the *Jeffersonian* which had suspended operations due to a lack of funds. Once again he was running a Republican paper in a strongly Democratic county and would do battle with both the rival *Courier* and with Copperheads.

In April, 1862 petitions were being circulated asking the Ohio Legislature to both prohibit blacks from moving to the state and expel those already living there. When Locke heard that a local man, Levi Flenner, whom he viewed as "worthless" was circulating such a petition, "The satire of the situation struck me at once," according to Locke. "The few negroes we had in

Findlay were hard-working, law-abiding men, and to remove them and leave Levi there was a preposterous outrage upon the fitness of things." Locke ridiculed the idea and Levi Flenner in a letter using his backwoods vernacular that he signed Petroleum V. Nasby—it's not exactly clear where he drew the inspiration for his pseudonym.

Titled "Letter From a Straight Democrat" it started

"The follerin petishun, the i jee uv wich wuz sejested bi me, hez bin cirkelated in Finlay durin the past wek...There is now fifteen niggers, men, wimen, and children, or ruther mail, femail, and yung in Findlay and yisterday another arove. I am bekoming alarmed fur if thay increse at this rate in suthin over sixty yeres they'll hev a majority in the town and may, ef thay git mene enuff, tirranize over us, even ez we air tirranizin over them. The danger is imminent! I imploar the peepil to wake up. Let us hold a mass meetin to taik this subgik into considerashun...Felow whites arous! The inemy is on to us!...Amerika fur white men! Petroleum V. Nasby,
Jest west uv Finley, Aprile the 20, 18sixty too."

Petroleum V. Nasby had been born. As the Civil War went on Locke would use him again and again as a vehicle to skewer people and ideas he opposed on local, state, and national issues. The fictional Nasby would hail from Wingert's Corners, a Crawford County crossroad known for its Southern sympathies. He would come to be the very antithesis of *noblesse oblige;* a self-indulgent, myopic, uneducated, bumpkin who longed for a bottomless jug of whiskey and an easy politically-appointed job, preferably one that would provide the opportunity to embezzle money. Nasby's primary interest in the Civil War was that it not inconvenience him in any way, shape or form.

When the draft was ordered there arose a variety of ways to evade it, medical excuses included, and Locke used Nasby to shame those using the latter: "I see in the papers last nite that the Government has institooted a draft...I know not wat uthers may do but ez for me, I can't go...I hev lost, sence Stanton's order to draft, the use of one eye entirely and hev kronic inflammashen in the other. My teeth is all unsound, my palit aint eggsactly rite, and I hev ed bronkeetis 31 yeres last Joon...I am rupchured in 9 places and am entirely enveloped with trusses. I hev verrykose veins, hev a white-swellin on wun leg and a fever sore on the uther; also wun leg is shorter than the tother, though I handle it so expert that nobuddy never noticed it..."

As the war went on and the enrollment officers were coming to Wingert's Corners, Locke sent Petroleum Nasby on an adventure. He fled to Toledo, borrowed a boat and rowed to Canada. Thinking it was safe to return he came back but was seized by federal authorities and sent off to war. He immediately deserted and joined a Confederate outfit called the "Loozeanner Pelikins," a circumstance Locke used to lampoon the Confederate army

The colonel in charge of the outfit went about procuring a Confederate uniform for Nasby. "Is Thompson dead yit?," said the colonel. "Not quite," sez the orderly. "Never mind," sez the kernel, "he cant git well uv that fever; strip off his uniform and give it to Nasby, and berry him." When Nasby received his new uniform, "I groaned innardly. There wuz a pair uv pants with the seat entirely torn away and wun leg gone below the knee, a shoe with the sole off, and the straw he had wrapped around the other foot, and a gray woolen shirt."

The colonel ordered Nasby to change. "Reluctantly, I pulled off my new dubble-soled boots and I wuz petrified to see the kernel kick off the slippers he wore and pull them on. I pulled off my pants—he put em on, and so on with every article uv dress I posssest, even to my warm overcoat and blankit." Nasby was then approached by three more officers who asked " ef I coodent git three more to desert." A wiser Nasby deserted his latest outfit at the first available opportunity and returned to Hancock County.

As in his first Nasby letter, Locke continued to ridicule those who feared black migration to Ohio. An 1863 letter exaggerated the number of blacks who had arrived in area counties since the start of the war.

```
Hankok............................................28,000
Wood........................................ ....84,200
Lorane [which is near Oberlin] .....103,000
[All uv which is studyin fer the ministry,
drawin cavelry captain's pay and rashens
till they gradoo8, incloodin 2 white servants each]
Sineky..........................................93,000
And so on, ad infinytum...
```

Locke never let up in his characterization of Nasby as a low-road type of guy as were, by extension, those Democrats and Copperheads who shared political common ground with him. At one point during the war Nasby was the preacher of a Wingert's Corners church. "This is a deliteful feeld uv labor. At the Corners they give me sich flooids ez I need at all the doggeries* but one, and at that one they trust me, wich amounts to the same thing. I hev borrid uv my flock over sixty dollars already. It is a rich feeld, and wun which will endoor much workin. My nose is deepnin in color every hour." [* an archaic term meaning "a low groghouse"]

Findlay residents read the letters with a mix of amusement and anger, depending on their politics, and Locke's reputation became known regionally. He became known nationally when he began to mail copies of the *Jeffersonian* to editors around the country who reprinted the Nasby letters in their own papers. And as those papers were sent to the Union troops in the field, Locke became popular with them as well. Many of them wrote him, Locke reprinting soldier's letters in almost every issue of the *Jeffersonian*.

Locke became well known in Washington as well, with perhaps his biggest fan there being Abraham Lincoln who not only committed passages of Nasby letters to memory but delighted in reading them aloud to cabinet members, members of Congress, family members, and White House visitors. Not everyone was so enamored, as Secretary of War Edwin M. Stanton was said to be annoyed to no small degree by Lincoln's renditions, considering the letters to be frivolous and beneath the dignity of the office of president. However Lincoln's admiration was unabashed, or as he put in a conversation with a senator, "For the genius to write these things I would gladly give up my office."

On the afternoon of April 14, 1865 Lincoln read aloud to a White House visitor from a personal copy of *The Nasby Papers*. That evening a bullet from the gun of John Wilkes Booth ended his life, making it possible that Nasby was the last thing read

Famed American cartoonist Thomas Nast's illustration of Petroleum V. Nasby holding court in one of his most familiar locations. (From "The Struggles of Petroleum V. Nasby").

by one of America's greatest presidents.

By that time Locke had severed his connections with the *Jeffersonian*, moving later in the year to Toledo where he became editor and owner of *Toledo Daily Blade*. During his stewardship he brought national repute to the *Toledo Weekly Blade*, increasing its circulation from 2,000 to an unheard of 80,000 in just three years.

In the post-Civil War years Locke continued to pen Nasby letters, and published several collections of them. In addition he toured the country on the lecture circuit and was considered a contemporary of fellow lecturer Mark Twain. He spent most of the 1870's in New York City as a newspaper editor and writer as well as dabbling in other fields. He returned to Toledo in 1879 to spend the final years of his life, dying in on February 15, 1888 after never fully recovering from a bout with tuberculosis a couple of years earlier. Upon his death, tributes poured into offices of the *Blade* from politicians, major newspapers around the country, and local newspaper subscribers lamenting the loss.

An Army colonel in Washington D.C. wrote, "The death of D.R. Locke closes a career of wider and more varied usefulness than comes to one man in ten million. His Nasby letters were worth more to the cause of the Union than an army corps. Their bitter ridicule found its way through the closest joints of the armor of pride, selfishness, ignorance and blind partisanship in which the enemies of the nation clothed themselves...He was the Cervantes who laughed away the right arm of the bogus chivalry of secession. We have all lost by the death of D.R. Locke, but the city of Toledo has lost vastly more than others."

CHAPTER VII

MAJOR GENERAL JAMES B. MCPHERSON

It was July 22, 1864 and both the weather and the fighting around Atlanta, Georgia were hot. Major General James Birdseye McPherson of Clyde, Ohio was checking the position of some of his troops as the campaign for Atlanta had ground into its third month. As he rode into the woods a line of soldiers dressed in gray suddenly arose and ordered him to halt. He paused, raised his hat as if giving salute, then wheeled his horse and dashed off at full gallop.

Seconds later, while bending low to ride under some tree branches, a musket ball slammed into his back and drove upward lodging near his heart. He fell hard to the ground and lay motionless while his orderly, who had been stunned when knocked to the ground by tree limbs, recovered and scrambled to his side. A Confederate captain rode up and demanded to know who was lying there. "Sir, it is General McPherson," choked the orderly, tears in his eyes. "You have killed the best man in our army." Major General James B. McPherson was the highest ranking Union soldier killed in the entire Civil War.

He was born near present-day Clyde in 1828 to one of Sandusky County's earliest settler families. At the age of 13 when his father fell into poor health, he walked five miles to Green Springs to work in a store and support his mother and three siblings. A voracious reader, he read the books on the shop's shelves and displayed a talent for drawing. The store's owner, who helped nurture him intellectually, was able to secure him an appointment to West Point, a remarkable achievement for someone coming from such simple circumstances. There he excelled academically, finishing first in his class when he graduated in 1853.

Major General James B. McPherson of Clyde, Ohio was the highest ranking Union officer killed in the Civil War. (National Archives).

He taught engineering at West Point for a year before working on engineering projects in the harbors of both New York and San Francisco, at the latter place meeting and falling in love with Emily Hoffman to whom he became engaged. In the winter of 1860-61 as the dark clouds of a looming Civil War were gathering on the horizon he wrote his mother from San Francisco, "My mind is perfectly made up and I can see that I have but one duty to perform, and that is to stand by the Union and the support of the general Government."

When the war started a few months later McPherson was a lieutenant of engineers. He initially was assigned to Boston in the summer of 1861 but began to long for service on the front lines. His skill in handling engineering projects early in the war impressed his superiors and he rose quickly in rank. In January, 1862 he had been assigned to General Ulysses S. Grant's Army of the Tennessee as the general's chief engineering officer.

He soon was directing troops in battle and had risen to the rank of brigadier general in May, then to major general (of volunteers) in October despite being only in his mid-thirties. He wrote his mother then, "Little did I think...when I saw you last November that I should ever be a Major General in the Army of the United States, but so it is." By this time he had earned not only the complete trust of General Grant but his close friendship as well.

In January, 1863 he was given command of the 17th Corps of the Army of the Tennessee which he led throughout the six week siege of Vicksburg which fell on July 4th. His compassionate treatment of the people of the occupied town did not always sit well with other Union officers and troops. His response was simply, "When the time comes that to be a good soldier, a man has to forget or overlook the claims of humanity, I do not want to be a soldier."

After Vicksburg, Grant wrote to Washington D.C. of McPherson, "He is one of the ablest engineers and most skillful Generals. I would respectfully but urgently recommend his promotion to the position of Brigadier General in the regular army." In August he was given that promotion and he remained in Vicksburg until March, 1864 when he was given a furlough to travel to Baltimore and marry his fiancee Emily.

He made it up the Mississippi River as far as Cairo, Illinois where a telegram from General William Tecumseh Sherman awaited: "Mac, it breaks my heart but you can't go now." One of the reasons Sherman needed McPherson back was his skill at settling feuds between West Point and non-West Point commanders which were a frequent problem. The wedding vows between McPherson and Emily would never be exchanged.

By May Union troops were on the march for Georgia and Atlanta with McPherson now commander of the Army of the Tennessee, as Ulysses Grant had gone east to take command of all the Union armies. The fight for Atlanta continued through

June and into July, the Union gaining ground but unable to deliver a finishing blow. On July 17th a former West Point classmate and friend who McPherson had personally tutored in school, John Bell Hood, was placed in charge of the Confederate forces protecting the city. When McPherson heard of the appointment of the aggressive General Hood he told his staff to be ready for an attack.

On July 21st Hood ordered a flanking movement against McPherson's left and rear. That attack came in the early afternoon of the 22nd, and noting a gap between his 16th and 17th Corps, McPherson was making the necessary adjustments when he rode into a line of Confederate skirmishers and was

A statue of General James B. McPherson marks his grave in McPherson Cemetery in Clyde, Ohio.

killed. When the news of his death reached General Sherman he ordered his body retrieved and brought to his headquarters. There, despite the fact that the battle continued to rage outside, a distraught Sherman paced about the room, tears dripping from his beard. When word of his death reached General Grant, it is said that he too wept bitterly.

A small memorial site with upturned cannon marks the spot of General James B. McPherson's death July 22, 1864. The site is in an aging neighborhood near downtown Atlanta.

Sherman said of his late friend, "I had expected him to finish the war. Grant and I are likely to be killed or set aside after failure to meet some popular expectations, and McPherson would have come into chief command at the right time to end the war. He had no enemies."

General McPherson's body was brought back to Clyde and he was buried on July 29th. After the funeral his 87-year-old grandmother, Lydia Slocum, wrote to General Grant thanking him for his friendship with and concern for her grandson. The commander of the Union army and future president wrote her back. "My Dear Madam, I am glad to know that the relatives of the lamented Major General McPherson are aware of the more than friendship that existed between him and myself. A Nation grieves at the loss of one so dear to our nation's cause It is a selfish grief, because the Nation had more to expect from him than from almost anyone living.

"I join in this selfish grief and the grief of personal love for the departed. He formed, for some time, one of my military family. I knew him well; to know him was to love. It may be some consolation to you, his aged grandmother, to know that every officer and every soldier who served under your grandson felt the highest reverence for his patriotism, his zeal, his great, almost unequaled ability, his amiability and all the many virtues that can adorn a commander. Your bereavement is great, but cannot exceed mine."

The loss of General McPherson was also felt by the author and poet Herman Melville who in the aftermath of his death penned, *A Dirge for McPherson*.

> Arms reversed and banners craped—
> Muffled drums;
> Snowy horse sable draped—
> McPherson comes.
> *But tell us, shall we know him more,*
> *Lost Mountain and lone Kenesaw?*
> Brave the sword upon the pall—
> A gleam in gloom;
> So a bright name lighteth all

McPherson's doom.
Bear him through the chapel door—
Let priest in stole
Pace before the warrior
Who led. Bell—toll!
Lay him down within the nave,
The Lesson read—
Man is noble, man is brave
But man's—a weed.
Take him up again and wend
Graveward, nor weep:
There's a trumpet that shall rend
This Soldier's sleep.
Pass the ropes the coffin round,
And let descend;
Prayer and volley—let it sound
McPherson's end.

True fame is his, for life is o'er—
Sarpedon of the mighty war.

CHAPTER VIII

BATTERY H, FIRST OHIO LIGHT ARTILLERY

Hints of dawn were in the eastern sky May 3 , 1863 during the Battle of Chancellorsville in Virginia when a portion of the Union army was ordered into retreat from a spot of ground called Hazel Grove. Covering the retreat, along with two other batteries was Battery H, First Ohio Light Artillery whose cannons roared. Before long the other two batteries had were ordered back, leaving Battery H to fight alone as Union troops poured past its position. Finally the order came for them to go and they escaped with the Confederates hot on their heels and losing three of their six guns in the process.

Later in the day, General Joseph "Fighting Joe" Hooker, commander of the Army of the Potomac, rode up to Battery H and said, "You have done splendidly. I saw you fight and did not expect you to get out. You have done your share." The above was small Union bright spot at Chancellorsville, a battle in which Confederate General Robert E. Lee gave the Union army a whipping and Hooker a thorough lesson in military strategy.

Chancellorsville was also one of over a dozen battles along with skirmishes and sieges fought by Battery H, a predominately Toledo and Lucas County company. The battery came about in the fall of 1861 at Camp Dennison in Cincinnati where a number of Lucas County volunteers had reported. There they were joined by some men from Marietta and Battery H was formed. The captain of the battery was a Marietta man named

James Huntington and the unit would also be known as Huntington's Battery as it customary for batteries to be also known by the name of its commander.

A light artillery regiment consisted of 12 batteries, A through M with six cannons each and, unlike an infantry regiment, individual batteries often fought in different venues. The majority of the First Ohio Light Artillery batteries fought in the deep south with only H and L fighting in the eastern theater only.

Battery H's first service was in the Shenandoah Valley campaigns in Virginia in the spring of 1862. It fought through the end of the war and when it returned home its flag bore the inscriptions of such battles as Winchester, Chancellorsville, Port Republic, Fredricksburg, and Gettysburg. When the war ended no reunions were held initially. As one former member put it, "At the close of the war we were tired of it and wanted to forget it." However in 1874 reunions began and out of these came the Gilbert Gaul painting of the battery in action at Cold Harbor, Virginia in June of 1864 seen on the cover of this book.

Stone honoring Battery H, First Ohio Light Artillery in Gettysburg National Military Park as it appeared at the time the park was established. (From "The Report of the Gettysburg Memorial Commission").

As the years passed the time took its toll and the number of former battery members attending reunions became smaller. At the last reunion in 1931 the sole surviving member, former private Adelbert Lewis, answered "Here."

Orin C. Dority

While Battery H did not write a history of their unit in action one member, Orin C. Dority, did keep an occasional journal. In the summer of 1862 Orin Dority joined the battery when an officer of the unit was in Toledo on a recruiting trip, the seventeen-year-old persuading his father to give consent. The wide-eyed farm boy traveled the first night with his fellow recruits to Columbus where they slept on the floor of the State Capitol Rotunda: "The hardest bed anytime in service," according to Dority. From there it was by train through the mountains and valleys of Virginia, then to Washington DC, then by boat down the Potomac River to Alexandria, Virginia where Battery H was in camp. He wrote home from there that he "had already seen what to me was worth more than a thousand dollars."

September found him on his first march, a "horrible green recruit. Three weeks ago I throwed down the old Sythe to try soldiering for three years unless sooner shot..." In December Battery H was taking part in the Battle of Fredericksburg, a Union defeat with heavy losses that featured charge after pointless charge by Union troops. "From what I can see it reminds me of driving sheep into a slaughter pen for they are getting mowed down like the grass of the meadow," Dority wrote.

The battery spent the winter of 1862-63 coping with the weather and buying tobacco from locals and selling it to soldiers. On May 3rd Dority described the battery's covering of the retreat of troops at Chancellorsville: "All the batteries were taken out of the field except ours. They say we have to cover the retreat from this nasty old place. 7:00 A.M. The Rebs are getting uneasy so they begin to sharpshoot a little and we not wishing to keep them waiting in suspense open fire on them with shell fixed so they would burst as soon as they left the piece." On May 5th Dority wrote "The roads are lined up with ambulances loaded with wounded. 8:00 P.M. All wet as water can make us and what is worse our blankets are soaking wet. We also lost our division commanders in our corps in the battle. General Whipple and General Berry both were killed...We have not heard yet but surmise that Hooker is badly defeated."

Dority's next entry was in July where Battery H found itself on Cemetery Hill during the Battle of Gettysburg. On July 3rd, the climactic day of the battle, the Confederates began with a daylight attack which was repulsed. "Then followed a silence of about three hours duration when the enemy opened up on us with one hundred pieces of artillery," Dority wrote. "It was at this time that the shells came crashing through the trees and gravestones at furious rates. They thought to drive us off of Cemetery Hill but that was no go for we had as many guns as they and could fire about as fast...This is the heaviest cannonading I ever heard." When the smoke cleared that day the Confederates had suffered a crushing defeat and the tide of the war had been turned.

Dority's next entry, other than a few remarks about life in camp in the winter of 1863-64, does not come until May. The fifth of that month found Battery H revisiting the battlefield at Chancellorsville. "Circumstances has again brought us upon this Bloody and long to be remembered spot," wrote Dority. "Just one year and two days ago, this morning dawned upon the boys of our Battery equally as beautiful as this day—yet how different the scene and circumstances."

"Then we were doomed to defeat with loss of many that has been with us so long and done their duty faithfully. Now we are at liberty to roam over the field and view the appalling sights that present themselves in any direction that one's fancy might choose to lead him. Hundreds of brave men fell upon that day and today they lay where they fell. They were buried and that is all you can say for them as only a few inches of dirt was thrown over them and now their bones lie bleaching in the sun, scattered about where the beasts of the forest left them...The forest that stood so thick is completely felled by the storm of bullets and shells that swept through them for two days and nights."

Battery H would be taking part in the General Grant's 1864 spring and summer campaigns in Virginia, scenes of terrible fighting and appalling losses on both sides as Grant was determined to take the Confederate capitol of Richmond while Robert E. Lee was just as determined to defend it.

On May 31st Battery H was at Cold Harbor, the place where they would later be memorialized on canvas. On June 3rd the final day of the battle, the battery fired continuously for two hours and despite having only four cannons, fired one thousand shells.

After fighting at Petersburg, Virginia in June, July found the battery on a boat sailing the waters of Chesapeake Bay to bolster the defenses at Washington DC. "It was here the swells of the ocean could be plainly felt and many of the boys were seasick," Dority wrote. "Some of them were afraid they would die while others were afraid they would not."

Their stay at the nation's capitol was short-lived however and after only a few days the battery was "doomed to go back to Petersburg...Back to our old camp once more and find things badly mixed up but here we are again just as we were six days ago. Have made a trip to Baltimore and Washington and back again—a ride of over five hundred miles. I will close by calling it quite an excursion."

In August Dority was ill and flat on his back in the hospital. "Oh, if I could but get what I would like to eat—some cheese, some peaches or a pickle, but they say it won't do to eat anything but a little gruel or coffee so I lay here and bite my lips thinking that when I am again well I will eat what I want."

By September Dority had rejoined Battery H, which spent the rest of the fall and early winter in various camps near Petersburg. In October Dority wrote, "hardly a day passes without having an artillery duel with the Rebel guns in our front." And as the onset of winter slowed down the fighting Dority wrote on December 25th, "It is Christmas but passes like another day as very few of us have money to get anything to eat anymore than usual."

In early spring of 1865 things heated up again as the Confederacy was in its final days. On the night of April 1st Battery H was engaged in heavy shelling as the final assault on Petersburg was to take place early the following morning. As the assault began, Battery H was called to the field. "The General in command sent for artillery to come out there and engage the Rebel Forts," Dority wrote. "We were among the first to go out and try the Johnnies right in the open field while they had good forts for protection. They made it rather warm for us to commence with but they cannot compete with Yankees in artillery firing. We soon knocked them out of time and captured it. We have since heard that General Lee was in the Fort and barely escaped our men."

The war was soon over for Battery H. On June 2nd they turned in their guns and ammunition in Washington and boarded flat cars for the rail journey home. They reached Baltimore where they were switched to box cars and where citizens waited with glasses of ice water, then on to Pittsburgh late at night where the women of the city had prepared a midnight supper. "Oh! but it was nice," Dority wrote. "The first real dandy meal in nearly three years."

From there it was to Cleveland, where discharge and another fine meal awaited, then on to Toledo where Mayor Charles M. Dorr and other city officials met them with a band and another feast. "There were speeches of welcome and everything in a blaze of glory, " Dority wrote. "After the dinner we formed and marched down Summit Street and back to the Middle Ground where we broke rank, shook the goodby hand and each went off their several ways."

On June 27th, 1867, Orin Dority, home on his farm that spread from what is now the northeast corner of Reynolds Road and Bancroft Street in Toledo wrote, "Since writing my last we have been mustered out and I have spent two years of peace and gratitude at home. In looking over my soldier's life I am pleased that I too have recorded a few facts which will help to clear up some doubts when kind memory is slightly effaced."

CHAPTER IX

THE DRUMMER BOY OF MISSION RIDGE

It was April, 1861 and war fever was running high as thousands of young men bid their families farewell and marched off to join the Union army. In Maumee, Ohio, a young German lad, John Kountz who had just turned 15, could only watch with envy as men who were his neighbors went to Toledo and Findlay to join the 14th and 21st Ohio regiments respectively.

Then in the summer of that year a German-speaking regiment composed of recent immigrants, the 37th Ohio, was mustered in Cleveland from various parts of the state with Lucas County contributing three companies and Maumee contributing Company G. When members of that company returned to Maumee at the end of September for a brief visit before departure for the field young Kountz told them how badly he wanted to serve. A Lieutenant Hamm sized him up and told him, "We will take you with us as a drummer."

His father, with great reluctance, gave his consent and two days later young Kountz bid him and his sister farewell and boarded a train and was off to the war, a drummer boy headed in harm's way. Kountz and the 37th Ohio spent 1862 taking part in battles and skirmishes in West Virginia, the lad surviving a serious illness and at one point rescuing a comrade who had fallen through the ice into a river. In 1863 the regiment moved south and fought in the Vicksburg campaign, suffering nearly 100 casualties. By this time the men of the regiment had grown very fond of "Johnny, the drummer boy." Their affection was due in part because his small stature reminded them of their children back home.

Later that year on the morning of November 25th, the 37th Ohio found itself at the base of Missionary Ridge in Chattanooga as it is now known and about to take part in the climatic third and final day of the battle for that city. Although Kountz was told by the regimental colonel to go to the rear with the other musicians he instead lingered. When the regiment made its charge up the ridge into a hail of gunfire he went with them, at one point casting aside his drum and grabbing the rifle of a slain comrade.

The regiment fell back under the withering fire and when it counted heads it realized their drummer boy was missing. A rifle ball had shattered his left leg and he lay bleeding badly in no-man's land, bullets from both sides whizzing over his head. Almost immediately Sergeant William Schmidt from his company volunteered to go get him and, despite the gunfire, raced forward. When he reached young Kountz the lad told him to save himself, that he was a goner anyway. However the sergeant threw him over his shoulder and carried him to safety. Schmidt later reported that he found the drummer boy nearer

Fifteen-year-old John Kountz of Maumee, Ohio went off to the Civil War as a drummer boy and returned as a hero. He was later awarded the Congressional Medal of Honor. (From "History of the Grand Army of the Republic.")

to enemy lines than any of the others wounded or killed.

Young Kountz was taken to a field hospital where he begged the surgeon to save his leg. He was put to sleep with chloroform and when he awoke he reached for his leg but it was gone, amputated at the hip. However his actions had earned him notoriety as he was now known as "The Drummer Boy of Mission Ridge."

It was February before he was able to walk on an artificial leg and leave the hospital on crutches. He finally made it home to Maumee in May, 1864, leaving as a boy and returning as a man. His homecoming was a sad one, however, as both his father and sister had died of illness while he was gone, his sister just a few weeks before, leaving him without family as his mother had died before the war.

But the loss of his leg and of his family left him undaunted. After attending school for a year he took a job in the Lucas County treasurer's office and in 1871 was elected county treasurer. He was later elected county recorder and after public life went into the insurance business.

However it was in post-war veterans activities that the one-time humble drummer boy would achieve national rank and repute. He joined the Grand Army of the Republic, the organization of Union veterans formed in 1866 (the last member died in 1956.) After heading a Toledo unit called the Forsythe Post he was elected commander of the Ohio Department in 1881. In 1884 he was elected to the position of commander-in-chief of the national G.A.R. and during his one-year term, membership in the group increased to over 50,000. He presided over the group's 1885 national encampment, held in Portland, Maine.

He also remained very involved in reunions of his old regiment, the 37th Ohio, telling them in an address at their ninth reunion in 1889, "I wish I could tell you how my heart rejoices as once again I look into your faces." At this reunion was recited the poem *The Drummer Boy of Mission Ridge*, a lengthy work that describes both the actions of John Kountz that day and of Sergeant Schmidt who came to his rescue.

In 1895 he was one of a number of soldiers, along with Sergeant Schmidt, awarded the Congressional Medal of Honor for meritorious service during the Civil War. It is believed that Kountz was the first Lucas County soldier so honored. There was some initial question, however, as to whether he had disobeyed orders the day he charged up the ridge but it was decided that he had, in fact, acted above and beyond the call of duty.

Kountz also served as secretary and historian of the Vicksburg National Military Park Commission and authored that body's 1901 official report of military units engaged in the campaign and battle of Vicksburg. His regiment, the 37th Ohio, had fought there.

One of his proudest moments came near the end of his life in 1908 when the national encampment of the Grand Army of the Republic was held in Toledo over Labor Day weekend. The city swelled with an estimated 200,000 visitors, 20,000 of them veterans, in an event Kountz helped bring about. A *Toledo Blade* profile of him at the time noted that "in all probability there is no man connected with the work of the Grand Army who is better known among the old soldiers from coast to coast than General Kountz."

In June, 1909 John Kountz died after being in failing health for about a year. His death was page one news, "Civil War Hero Answers Call," pretty high praise for a onetime scared little drummer boy.

Note: The poem "The Drummer Boy of Mission Ridge" appears in the appendix.

CHAPTER X

DEATH COMES HOME

While Civil War soldiers in the field were subject to various deprivations and hardships there was mental and emotional suffering for their families back home. And that was the daily knowledge that word could come at any time that their son, or brother, or husband, or father had died in the war. The news most often came by mail: a letter from a far away place with unfamiliar handwriting and ripped open with trembling hands. Inside was the dreaded word they would never see their loved one again, words that were like a high, arching shell reaching from the battlefield and exploding in their midst.

Just such a shell exploded in the world of the family of Levi and Harriet Munson. According to the 1860 census they were a farming couple with four children west of Toledo when the war broke out the following year. Their oldest child, Eliakim, bade his parents and siblings farewell in September, 1861 and came to Toledo and signed on as a private in the 14th Ohio Volunteer Infantry. His short life came to an end two years later on September 19, 1863 when was he was killed on the first day of the Battle of Chickamauga. The news of his death may have been especially devastating as a brief, battle-related article that appeared in the September 25th edition of the Toledo Daily Blade reported: "Casualties in the 14th Ohio—none killed."

Eliakim was probably buried where he fell. Levi and Harriet

Munson subsequently erected a stone in the memory of their son in nearby Wolfinger Cemetery, a small, historic burial ground now surrounded by the tall trees of Secor Metropark. Over time they were laid to rest there too, next to the monument they placed for their first-born child.

Another who felt the anguish of a loved one put in harm's way by the Civil War was the poet Walt Whitman. In December, 1862 he rushed to the front in Virginia when he saw the name of his brother George on a list of wounded. Once there he stayed, working in and visiting army and field hospitals until health problems led him to return home in the summer of 1864. His observations and experiences led him to a write a number of Civil War poems, an event he termed a "strange, sad war." One of his efforts, *Come Up From the Fields, Father*, was situated, like the Munson family, on a family farm in Ohio

This stone in Wolfinger Cemetery in Secor Metropark west of Toledo memorializes Eliakim Munson. It reads "Eliakim Munson, A Private in Co. F 14th Reg't O.V.I. Killed at Chickamauga, Geo. Sept. 19, 1863 Aged 20 YRS. 5 MS. 15 DAS."

in the autumn, and perhaps reflects their ordeal.

Come up from the fields, father, here' s a letter from our Pete,
And come to the front door mother, here's a letter from thy dear son.
Lo, 'tis autumn,
Lo, where the trees, deeper green, yellower and redder,
Cool and sweeten Ohio's villages with leaves fluttering in the moderate wind,
Where apples ripe in the orchards hang and grapes on the trellis'd vines,
(Smell you the smell of the grapes on the vines?
Smell you the buckwheat where the bees were lately buzz-ing?)
Above all, lo, the sky so calm, so transparent after the rain, and with wonderous clouds.
Below too, all calm, all vital and beautiful, and the farm pros-pers well.
Down in the field all prospers well,
But now from the fields come father, come at the daughter's call,
And come to the entry mother, to the front door come right away.
Fast as she can she hurries, something is ominous, her steps trembling,
She does not tarry to smooth her hair nor adjust her cap.
Open the envelope quickly,
O this is not our son's writing, yet his name is sign'd,
O a strange hand writes for our dear son, O stricken mother's soul!
All swims before her eyes, flashes with black, she catches the main words only,
Sentences broken, *gunshot wound in the breast, cavalry skir-mish, taken to hospital,*
At present low, but will soon be better.
Ah now the single figure to me,
Amid all teeming and wealthy Ohio with all its cities and farms,

Sickly white in the face and dull in the head, very faint,
By the jamb of a door leans.
Grieve not so, dear mother, (the just-grown daughter speaks through her sobs,
The little sisters huddle around speechless and dismay'd).
See dearest mother, the letter says Pete will soon be better.
Alas poor boy, he will never be better, (nor may-be needs to be better, that brave and simple soul,)
While they stand at home at the door he is dead already,
The only son is dead.
But the mother needs to be better,
She with thin form presently drest in black,
By day her meals untouch'd, then at night fitfully sleeping, often waking,
In the midnight waking, weeping, longing with one deep longing,
O that she might withdraw unnoticed, silent from life escape and withdraw,
To follow, to seek, to be with her dead son.

CHAPTER XI

GENERAL RUTHERFORD B. HAYES

The only president to hail from northwest Ohio also wore the general's star in the Civil War. Rutherford Birchard Hayes was born in Delaware, Ohio in 1822. He was graduated from Kenyon College 20 years later. From there he went to Harvard Law School where he earned his degree in 1845. In 1846 he began a law practice in the growing river town of Lower Sandusky, now Fremont. Business was slow for the young attorney however and he moved to Cincinnati in 1849.

His law practice thrived there as well as his personal life, as he married Lucy Webb in 1852 (she would later be the first First Lady to have a college degree). Through the 1850's he gained a reputation as an accomplished defense lawyer and in 1858 was appointed to the post of city solicitor. In April, 1861 the successful and respected Rutherford B. Hayes had just returned to private practice when the Confederates attacked Fort Sumter and his life changed dramatically as it did for so many at that time. In May he wrote in his diary, "I would prefer to go into it if I knew I was to die, or be killed in the course of it, than live through and after it without taking any part in it."

Although he and Lucy had three sons and she was pregnant with a fourth, he dissolved his law practice and contacted the governor and offered his services to the war effort. He was made a major in the 23rd Ohio Volunteer Infantry, a regiment recruited from the northern and northeastern counties of the state, and spent the summer at Camp Chase in Columbus learning the military life along with his green troops. One of those soldiers was a young private named William McKinley, meaning the 23rd Ohio had on its roster not one but two future presidents.

By fall Major Hayes and the 23rd Ohio were in the mountains of Virginia where in October he was promoted to lieutenant colonel and soon after given command of the regiment. His devotion in the Union cause was unshakable as he wrote in his diary, "My belief in this war is as deep as any faith can be."

He would spend the bulk of the in war Virginia and West Virginia— which was cleaved from the from the former and given statehood in 1863—doing less glamorous work such as fighting small battles, rooting out guerrillas, patrolling the rugged hills, and keeping Southern civilian sympathizers in check. However one of the advantages of being in the Virginias for the family man Hayes was the proximity of his loved ones.

In September, 1862 during the Antietam campaign, one of the few occasions he fought outside the Virginias, he was leading the 23rd Ohio in the Battle of South Mountain when a bullet tore through his left arm leaving a gaping hole and breaking, but not splintering, the bone. It would be the most serious of the five wounds received during the war. While his two-month convalescence was a painful one he was able to return to Ohio and spend time with his family.

In January, 1863, now a full colonel, he was made a commander of the First Brigade consisting of the 23rd Ohio, two other regiments, three cavalry companies and a battery. He and was joined in his unit's winter camp near Charleston by Lucy and their two older boys. For the next two months he delighted in watching his boys enjoy the camp life while Lucy rode horseback and fished the Kanawha River. The coming of spring saw little action in the area and in June Lucy came again, this time bringing all the boys including eighteen-month-old Joe of whom Hayes had seen little of as he had been born after the war started. But this would become a sad visit as little Joe came down with dysentery and died.

In July Colonel Hayes and two regiments raced up the Ohio

River in steamboats taking part in the pursuit of Confederate General John Hunt Morgan and his band of raiders and capturing about 200 of them. The rest of the year was relatively quiet with Hayes writing Lucy in August, "I ride about, read novels, newspapers and military books and sleep." Later in the year he was flattered when friends offered to push for his promotion to brigadier general but said, "I'd prefer to be a good colonel to being one of the poor generals."

Colonel Hayes spent a quiet winter and again was joined by Lucy and the two older boys. However things would heat up in 1864. In May, Hayes and the First Brigade were part of a charge up a steep, wooded hill called Cloyd's Mountain, overrunning rebel positions. In a short but furious fight the brigade lost 250 killed or wounded, nearly half of them from the 23rd Ohio. The summer months that followed were filled with hard marching and fighting as Union troops rooted out Confederates from the valleys of Virginia.

In September, 1864 during the heat of the Battle of Opequon Creek during the Shenandoah Valley campaign Hayes found himself in a major predicament. He was at the head of his brigade while charging toward a rebel line and battery when they unexpectedly came across a wide muddy creek or swamp which halted the advance and created a moment of confusion.

The colonel knew they could not stand there exposed to enemy fire and retreating was unthinkable. He knew he would have to lead his men across himself.

"Hayes, with the instinct of a soldier, at once gave the word 'Forward" and spurred his horse right into the swamp. Horse and rider plunged at first nearly out of sight, but Hayes struggled on till the beast sank hopelessly into the mire. Then dismounting, he waded to the further bank, climbed to the top and beckoned with his cap to the men to follow. In the attempt to obey many were shot or drowned, but a sufficient number crossed the ditch to form a nucleus for the brigade; and Hayes still leading, they climbed the bank and charged the battery. The enemy fled in great disorder and Hayes reformed his men and resumed the advance. The passage of the slough was at the crisis of the fight and the rebels broke on every side in confusion."

The day ended with a resounding Union victory. Colonel Hayes, who after the battle took over for a wounded division commander, led the division in two more battles in the Shenandoah Valley campaign and for his efforts was commissioned in October a brigadier general of volunteers. By that time things were winding down in the Virginias theater and though General Hayes finished the war as a brevet major general of volunteers, he did not fight in battle as a general.

General Rutherford B. Hayes of Fremont went on to become the only U.S. president to hail from northwestern Ohio. (Rutherford B. Hayes Presidential Center, Fremont, Ohio).

The end of the war did not mean the end of duty, even briefly, for Rutherford B. Hayes. For he had been chosen in the 1864 election as congressman from Cincinnati while still in the army. He had been approached in the summer of 1864 about running but declined saying, "An officer fit for duty who at this crisis would abandon his post to electioneer for a seat in Congress ought to be scalped." He was nominated and elected anyway, despite his refusal to campaign.

He took his congressional seat in 1865 after the war was over, was reelected in 1866, then served two, two-year terms as Ohio's governor, returning in 1873 to Fremont to live at Spiegel Grove, the 25 acre wooded grounds and mansion of his uncle, an estate he would inherit the following year. But politics came calling again and he was elected to a third term of governor, taking office in January, 1876. Later that year he was nominated for president by the Republican Party, winning the office in a disputed election decided by a special commission. As promised he served only one term despite pressure from many to reconsider his decision.

He came home for good to Fremont in 1881 to Spiegel Grove, spending the remaining twelve years of his life working on behalf of countless worthy causes. He died there in 1893 and is buried on the grounds alongside his beloved wife Lucy.

CHAPTER XII

LIMA GOES TO WAR

It was a warm and sunny April day in Lima, Ohio, in 1861 when word began to crackle through the streets and the open windows of homes and businesses. Fort Sumter had been attacked and war was now upon the nation. Before long an American flag hung high from a wire strung between Ashton Hall and the Allen County Courthouse and a buzzing crowd began to gather on the courthouse lawn.

A platform was improvised and a local minister and other dignitaries delivered stirring appeals to patriotism. In the coming days scores of Lima and area men would make the decision to leave behind friends, family, and all that was familiar and march off to war.

In less than two weeks a company of over 100 men was organized and preparing to leave for camp in Columbus, destined to become part of the 20th Ohio Volunteer Infantry. And on the day of their departure the scene "eclipsed anything of the kind known in the history of Lima," reported the *Lima Weekly Gazette.*

"By daylight our people were stirring and before eight o'clock they began to come from the country. At noon and from there to four o'clock not less than four thousand people were on our streets with anxious faces...the most perfect order was maintained, notwithstanding the immense crowd, and everything passed off without accident."

When the 3 p.m. train of the Dayton and Michigan Railroad pulled in to take the men to Columbus the station was a sea of humanity. "The Depot and grounds were all alive with people when the train arrived and the scenes of leave taking and farewell caused the tears to flow from many a manly heart," the newspaper reported.

In Columbus one of the Lima volunteers wrote home from camp. "Columbus presents a wonderful scene to one who has been accustomed to peace and the calm of the rural home. Hurried preparations for the war are seen on every side. The beat of the drum, the march of the military companies, the constant huzzahs for the Union, the singing of the Star Spangled Banner, and the curses upon traitors all present a novel condition of things." He marveled at the societal range of those who volunteered from Lima and Allen County such as a professor, a judge, legislators, and members of the clergy and of the bar. "Hence the present manifestation is not the wild rushing together of madmen, but the calm determination of men of the highest intelligence, having the highest end in view that could animate a nation."

For a time Allen County volunteers could organize locally as Camp Lima was established in the city in the summer of 1862 and spread over 15 acres of ground. In August of that year 1600 men were in camp marching and drilling and two full regiments were organized there.

In April, 1861 volunteers lined up in Public Square in Lima to fight for the Union in the Civil War. (Allen County (Ohio) Historical Society).

However all the noble intentions and high ideals were no insulation from the cruel realities of war. In the memoirs of a Lima woman there was an incident recorded, one repeated countless thousands of times across the country. In the spring of 1862, "I saw there was a commotion and from the Post Office came the sound of a woman weeping bitterly. It proved to be Hattie Armstrong...A letter had been received by her which was addressed in a strange handwriting. She tore it open with trembling hand and read the cruel blow that her brother had been shot thro' the head and instantly killed..." Her brother, Captain Mart Armstrong, had been killed on the first day of the Battle of Shiloh and was the first well known Lima resident to die in the war. His grieving father went to Tennessee and retrieved his body and brought it home to lay in state in Ashton Hall, "The Warrior at Rest" emblazoned on the canopy over the coffin.

When the Civil War came to an end Lima and Allen County, with a total population of less than 20,000, had sent nearly 2,000 soldiers to the Union cause. About 10% never returned.

In the early days of the Civil War regiments could organize locally at Camp Lima, the headquarters of which is seen in this Fall, 1862 photo. The short-lived camp had been abandoned by the end of that year. Those pictured include Ohio Governor Thomas L. Young and Colonel James Cunningham. (Allen County (Ohio) Historical Society).

organized to protect men against theft and everyone convicted of stealing was brought up and whipped." Internal order was consequently restored to the prison, Reynolds noted.

The captain continued his work in the hospital as the summer of 1864 and its scorching heat wore on. On August 4th the hospital admitted 400 men and, with room for only 200, the rest laid outside until death opened up a bed. The prisoners were now dying at the rate of nearly 100 per day, mostly of starvation or related effects, and were buried in trenches, 75 in each trench. Rations continued to be scant and Captain Reynolds by this time had shrunk to a skeletal 75 pounds.

Some relief came when a Catholic priest from Savannah visited and distributed $100,000 to the prisoners that had been collected. In addition he gave the hospital several months supply of flour which saved hundreds of lives. Another thing that saved lives was medicine, or a lack thereof, according to Reynolds. When supplies of medicine ran low, whiskey was substituted. "I know it is a fact that *always* when medicine ran short and whiskey was supplied freely, the percentage of mortality decreased, " Reynolds wrote. "Another advantage whiskey had over the other medicine was it was not near so hard to take."

Of the various units that guarded the prison, it was the ones who had never seen battle that were the cruelest, Reynolds noted. There was a line near the stockade wall called the Dead Line. Under prison rules any inmate crossing that line could be shot. A unit called the Home Guards, which had never seen action, rarely let an opportunity to shoot a prisoner slip by, according to Captain Reynolds. On the other hand when the guard posts were manned by members of the 55th Georgia Regiment, which had seen battle and had spent time in a Union prison in Columbus, Ohio, the opposite was true. "One day two brothers, walking skeletons, tired of life, joined hands and stepped boldly over the Dead Line hoping to be shot," he wrote. Not only did the guards from the 55th refuse to fire but one of their officers talked to the despondent men and led them back across the line.

By the end of September, 1864 the number of deaths at the prison approached 10,000, according to Captain Reynolds.

Many of those dying refused to come to the hospital, preferring to remain in the filthy conditions of the prison where at least they could die among friends. In October a poem found on the body of a dead prisoner, dated a few days before his death, reflects his bitterness and despair:

> From out our prison gate
> There's a graveyard near at hand
> Where lie ten thousand Union men
> Beneath the Georgia sand
> Scores on scores are laid beside them
> As day succeeds today
> And thus it will ever be
> Till they all shall pass away
> And the last can say when dying
> With upturned gazing eye
> Both love and faith are dead at home
> They have left us here to die.

The Union prisoners who died at Andersonville were buried in trenches, 75 per trench. (National Archives).

The suffering of Captain Reynolds and his fellow prisoners continued through the end of the war; prisoner exchanges were resumed March, 1865, mere weeks before war's end. To him Andersonville was "a dark spot, a fearful whirlpool into which were drawn many of the best and bravest of youths to be tormented, tempted, bruised, beaten and starved by so slow a process as to lengthen their miseries till they should seek and welcome death...Future generations will have its history to remind them of it, and they can only think of it with silent horror and wonder that such things could really have existed in this enlightened and Christian age."

After the war Charles Reynolds returned home and regained his health. He was married and built up a successful real-estate and insurance business while serving in several city of Napoleon and Henry County offices. He died in 1925 and was buried in Glenwood Cemetery in Napoleon.

CHAPTER XIV

THE SLAVERY DEBATE

At the outbreak of the Civil War, views on slavery varied widely in the North. The range of views on the issue were reflected in several incidents in the history of the 21st Ohio as recalled by Arnold McMahan, a captain and later colonel in the regiment, who was very much against slavery and whose beliefs would be put to the test.

When Fort Sumter was fired on, igniting the Civil War, a patriotic fervor erupted in the North primarily over protecting the integrity of the Union, according to Captain McMahan. "The slavery question so far as our regiment was concerned had no consideration whatever at that time."

As the war went on and the regiment moved south, the soldiers got their first close exposure to slavery when they occupied Huntsville, Alabama in April, 1862. "This is the most lovely country in the world; the land of the magnolia and the home of the mocking bird," Captain McMahan wrote. "But it was in the heart of the slave power, and here we saw the perfection of systematic slavery."

The soldiers overall tended to be sympathetic toward the slaves, according to Captain McMahan. "There were very few men in the regiment who would deceive the slaves. They were always told that we could not take care of them and that the land of freedom was directly under the north star." Some slaves, however, were hidden in the tents of soldiers when some plantation owners came to retrieve them. Colonel Jesse Norton, commander of the regiment, ordered them turned over, "to the great disgust of the Yankees," McMahan wrote.

This same Colonel Norton soon got into trouble for consorting with plantation owners which led to his arrest and eventual resignation from the military by the end of the year. "Thus while Colonel Norton had no clear convictions on the slave question, his affiliation with pro-slavery men who were also enemies of his government worked to his ruin, and deprived the regiment of its commander and original organizer," noted Captain McMahan.

Norton was replaced by Lieutenant Colonel James Neibling who was a "pronounced pro-slavery man," according to McMahan, "and did not hesitate to voluntarily detain slaves in the county jail until their masters came for them." In August a lieutenant, when ordered by Neibling to return a slave he had hired as a servant, resigned as he did not want to "serve under a Colonel who returned slaves to their masters." His resignation was never acted on. That same month a captain refused a direct order from Neibling to turn over a slave he had hired as a servant.

Captain McMahan seethed over the role the regiment was playing in detaining fugitive slaves. When he was appointed officer of the day for the first time in two months, he decided to do something about it. "I made up my mind that when I went on duty the next morning I would break up the slave trade in the regiment for twenty-four hours at least, and my success surprised me." The county jail held a number of slaves being held on no criminal charges and McMahan was determined to release them.

He assembled a guard of men and informed Colonel Neibling of his intent. He answered, "Sir, I order you not to do it." Captain McMahan replied, "Colonel, would you be so good as have charges preferred against them." Neibling exploded in rage and ordered McMahan to return to his quarters, that he was under arrest.

Word spread through the regiment and the initial reaction was that Captain McMahan, who was a disciplinarian and not popular among the men, had gotten what he deserved. However as the day went on that reaction changed dramatically and the regiment was in a state of near rebellion against Neibling. By sundown, all the slaves had been released by Neibling himself who then rescinded McMahan's arrest. A committee of officers prepared a list of charges to be made against Neibling but they never were formally made and the matter eventually died down.

The slavery debate within the regiment continued until the Battle of Chickamauga in September, 1863. The death and suffering there forged a unity of belief that had not previously existed. After the battle the slavery question "was never heard of in the regiment again," wrote McMahan. "The result of that battle provoked a spirit of determination in our men that never could yield until the South was overthrown." In addition, after the battle, a regimental lieutenant became "the first officer to muster a negro into the service of his company rolls and give the slave the protection of the government."

CHAPTER XV

Congressman James M. Ashley

It was the last day of January, 1865 and a chill wind swept through the streets of Washington D.C. But on Capitol Hill the atmosphere was anything but cold as members of the House of Representatives, in front of a packed gallery, engaged in final debate on legislation that would, in effect, become the 13th amendment to the Constitution banning slavery.

In the center of the highly charged swirl was Representative James M. Ashley of Toledo, an abolitionist who not only had authored the original legislation but had walked the political point to bring it this far. The Senate had already passed the amendment the previous April but a vote in June by the House had fallen short of the two-thirds majority needed for passage. And at the close of debate that January day members of the House voted on a measure to reconsider the June action. The measure passed, but at a number still short of the two-thirds that would be needed for the actual amendment and a buzz rippled through the gallery.

Ashley was advised to seek a postponement but he refused, imbued perhaps with the quiet confidence a morally strong stance can provide. He had led the fight in the House to ban slavery throughout the Civil War and was not going to back down now. A roll call vote proceeded and one by one the Representatives stood and cast their vote. When the vote concluded an absolute hush settled over the House. The clerk announced the tally—119 yes, 56 no, 8 abstentions. It had passed by three votes.

The House erupted in pandemonium. Members threw their hats in the air and women in the gallery waved handkerchiefs and shouted, "Hurrah for Freedom." A jubilant James Ashley raced from the House and rode a carriage to the office of Secretary of War Edwin Stanton to inform him of the result. He then wired the *Toledo Commercial* newspaper, "Glory to God in the highest! Our country is free!"

Unlike David Ross Locke, Ashley did not receive his anti-slavery views at home. Born in 1824, he spent his childhood along the Ohio River in Portsmouth, Ohio. His father was a stern, devoutly religious but pro-slavery itinerant preacher. A young James Ashley frequently accompanied his father on his preaching circuit in Kentucky and Virginia which gave him the opportunity to witness the practice of slavery first hand. He was repelled by what he saw, along with what he considered to be his father's hypocrisy on the issue. He also became deeply suspicious of the organized religions of the time, many of which supported, or at least did not oppose, slavery.

At the age of 14 when his father pressured him to follow him in his ministerial path, Ashley rebelled and left home. Over the next few years he worked on Ohio River steamers, which provided further opportunity to view the injustices of slavery, and he lived with an abolitionist Quaker family who were friends of his mother. His anti-slavery outlook continued to harden.

Through the 1840's Ashley worked a variety of jobs in Portsmouth and was involved in helping runaway slaves. He also spoke out against the Fugitive Slave Act of 1850 which did not make him popular in Portsmouth, a town with a fair amount of pro-slavery sentiment. In 1851 he decided to move north to St. Paul, Minnesota but stopped in Toledo on the way and decided to stay.

In the 1850's he owned a couple of general stores in Toledo and became involved in local politics in a decade that saw the nation increasingly divided on the slavery issue. In 1856, while campaigning on behalf of the local Republican candidate for the U.S. House of Representatives, he gave an ardent anti-slavery speech before a throng near Montpelier, Ohio that ended,

"It cannot be that this long, dark night of shame and crime will endure forever...come what may, American slavery must be destroyed!" This put him at the forefront of what at the time was considered radical abolitionism.

In 1858 Ashley decided to run for the House seat himself and ran a vigorous campaign giving nearly 100 speeches, mostly in Methodist churches. Because of his strong views he was often heckled and once while speaking was struck in the head by a live goose thrown through a window. During another speech he told a heckler to be quiet or leave, to which the heckler responded by daring Ashley to throw him out. The candidate leaped down from the stage, grabbed the heckler by the collar, dragged him to the door and did just that. The incident served to increase the size of the crowds at future speeches because people wanted to see what this hands-on politician might do next.

In the 1858 election, Ashley won a tight race, winning by around 500 votes out of over 20,000 cast. In 1859 he traveled to

Congressman James M. Ashley of Toledo was an ardent abolitionist who pursued legislation banning slavery during the Civil War. (National Archives).

Virginia to witness the execution of the abolitionist John Brown, then met with and comforted Brown's wife afterward. In 1860 he was reelected, beating Toledoan James B. Steedman who would go on to be a Civil War general, and campaigned hard for Abraham Lincoln. In late 1860 and early 1861, as the country was ready to split apart at the seams, he opposed any Congressional conciliatory or compromising measures toward the South, convinced that war was inevitable and, for that matter, necessary.

In a June, 1861 letter to the *Toledo Daily Blade* he wrote, "our army should sweep before its triumphant march every armed traitor from the Potomac to the Gulf, and hold and occupy the rebellious States as provinces, if necessary, until a reconstruction by Union and patriotic men is made possible."

In 1862 Ashley introduced a bill in the House that abolished slavery and extended land and voting rights to slaves but got nowhere as these ideas were considered to be too radical for the time. Later in the year he was reelected to his seat, beating back a tough challenge from Toledoan and future Supreme Court Chief Justice Morrison R. Waite.

In December, 1863 Ashley again introduced a bill abolishing slavery which was voted on the following June, failing to get a two-thirds majority. Ashley himself ended up voting against the bill in a parliamentary move which would allow him to bring it up again. In the following months he relentlessly lobbied Representatives who had voted against it, knowing he needed around ten to change their minds.

In early January, 1865 he brought the resolution before the House again, quoting Abraham Lincoln, "If slavery is not wrong, nothing is wrong." This put in motion the vote of January 31st and the eventual constitutional banishment of slavery. While the final wording of the 13th amendment differed somewhat from Ashley's original text, it's intent did not. Newspapers praised his efforts, including the *National Anti-Slavery Standard* which wrote, "The credit belongs principally to Mr. Ashley of Ohio. He has been at work the whole session and it is his management that secured passage of the Joint Resolution."

Ashley would win one more term in 1866, becoming deeply

involved in the efforts to impeach President Andrew Johnson, a role for which history records him a more prominent place. His aggressive and uncompromising pursuit of President Johnson cast him in disfavor with the voters and he was defeated in the 1868 election. In 1869 he was appointed governor of the Montana territory by President Ulysses Grant, a position that lasted less than a year after he fell into disfavor with the president for a combination of reasons, his outspokenness included.

He returned to Ohio and practiced law and continued his involvement in politics, campaigning heavily for Horace Greeley, President Grant's opponent in the 1872 election. When Greeley was badly defeated, Ashley's political career was, for all intents and purposes, over. He would run for his old congressional seat in 1890 and 1892 but lose both times.

Where Ashley did find post-political life success was in the railroad business. Working with his sons James and Henry, he opened the first railroad between Toledo and Ann Arbor, Michigan in 1878. Eleven years later that line extended across the lower peninsula to the Lake Michigan shore near Traverse City and was known as the Toledo, Ann Arbor and Northern Michigan Railroad.

In 1893 he was honored by the Afro-American League of Tennessee for his anti-slavery efforts, the president of that group saying in part, "We come not as partisans, but as freedmen and citizens, the immediate beneficiaries of the crowning act of Mr. Ashley's noble life."

In the summer of 1896, in declining health and suffering from diabetes, he became ill while on a fishing trip in Michigan and died of a heart attack in September in an Ann Arbor hospital and was buried in Toledo's Woodlawn Cemetery. A plaque on the Ashley family monument there notes his accomplishments in public service and business and also states he is "recognized by common consent and honored as the leader in Congress of the battle for the adoption of the thirteenth amendment to the Constitution of the United States."

CHAPTER XVI

THE COLORS MUST STAND

Charging over open ground into a haze of murderous gunfire with resulting high casualties was an all too common feature of Civil War battles. One of those charges was made at Jonesboro, Georgia on September 1, 1864 during the Atlanta campaign and the Union regiments fighting there that day included the 38th Ohio Volunteer Infantry. The regiment was organized at Defiance, Ohio in September, 1861 with the large majority of the unit coming from both Defiance County and adjacent Williams County.

It had been a hot and blood-soaked summer in Georgia as Union troops clawed their way to the outskirts of Atlanta, the heart of the Confederate war machine. And as September dawned, the two sides were lined up near the village of Jonesboro, south of the city, the Confederates by this time reeling and demoralized, a fact sensed perhaps by the Union soldiers.

Late in the afternoon after an initial Union thrust was repulsed, the battle began in earnest with a wild Union charge through a cotton field toward Confederate positions as described by a Union officer: "Generals, Colonels, Majors, Captains and privates all had to go forward together over that open field facing and drawing nearer to death at every step we took, our horses crazy, frantic with the howling shells, the rattling of canister and the whistling of bullets, ourselves delirious with the wild excitement of the moment and thinking only of getting over those breastworks...we left hundreds of bleeding comrades behind us at every step but not at one instant did that line hesitate."

Taking part in that charge was the 38th Ohio whose color guard would pay a steep price. First, Corporal Randall bore the regimental flag and was almost immediately killed. The colors were then seized by Corporal Baird who minutes later lay dead. Then Corporal Strawser grabbed the flag and was struck with a bullet, leaving him on the ground severely wounded. Seeing the colors on the ground, regimental commander Colonel Choate was in the act of reaching for them when he received what would prove be a mortal wound. Then came Corporal Donze carrying a wounded captain to the rear when the captain was struck again, killing him, thus making his removal from the field no longer necessary. The corporal

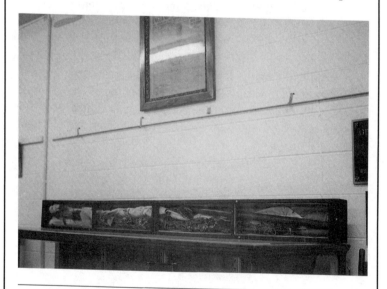

The flag of the 38th O.V.I. from Williams and Defiance counties, seen above, was planted on Confederate works during the Battle of Jonesboro in September, 1864, but not before four color bearers were killed or seriously wounded. (Williams County Historical Society, Montpelier, Ohio).

turned and saw the colors on the ground, seized them and forced his way forward and planted the bloodstained flag on the Confederate breastworks as Union troops rolled over the rebel lines.

When darkness finally brought an end to the fighting, 42 members of the 38th Ohio lay dead and another 108 had been wounded; total Union casualties were 1,275. In addition to the loss of Colonel Choate, only one of the 38th Ohio's five man color guard escaped being killed or wounded. But he, Corporal Brooks, was not untouched as he counted five bullet holes in his clothing. Their suffering was not in vain, however, as during the night and the next day the Confederates hastily abandoned the city of Atlanta. And early in the morning of September 3rd, President Lincoln received a message he had been waiting all summer for, "Atlanta is ours and fairly won," and the Civil War was one large step closer to being over.

In the years that followed the war the regimental flag was held in particular reverence by surviving members of the 38th Ohio during their reunions. "Though a small and tattered portion remains, which is faded and bloodstained, it is to them more beautiful than on the day when they received it with its bright colors and silken folds," according to a history of the regiment. "It is the sacred memories that cluster round it that make it beautiful."

CHAPTER XVII

ESCAPE FROM ANDREWS RAID

The Civil War was in full rage in 1862 as rain fell from a gray morning sky on the 12th day of April in Big Shanty, Georgia. There, 22 men boarded the northbound train the "General," Union men dressed as civilians. Their mission: to hijack the train and destroy track and telegraph lines as they charged north, eventually reaching Union territory. The line, the Western & Atlantic Railroad, linked Atlanta and Chattanooga and was vital to Confederate interests.

It was a bold mission and one ultimately doomed to failure. The 21 soldiers and their civilian leader, a contraband merchant named James Andrews, had to abandon the train after eight hours and 87 miles and all were eventually captured. The event came to be known as Andrews Raid, also known as Mitchel's Raid for the general who sanctioned the event. The sheer daring and drama of the mission has made it one of the more famed events of the Civil War with hundreds of accounts being written about it over the years as well as three motion pictures.

Almost all of the Raiders were from Ohio and of those 12 were from northwestern Ohio including five from Wood County. Among those five were John "Alf" Wilson from Haskins and Mark Wood from Portage, privates in the 21st Ohio. Wilson wrote a lengthy account of his adventure, initially a series for the "Wood County Sentinel" newspaper in the late 1870's then published in book form in 1880. Most of his book concerns not the raid itself but the months that followed, an incredible story of both the sheer capacity of human endurance and of the will to survive.

On the afternoon of April 12th it was clear the Andrews Raiders were in trouble. The General was running out of fuel and despite damage done to the track and obstacles thrown in its path, a Confederate train driven by a relentless conductor was pulling nearer. When musket balls from the soldiers on the pursuing train started bouncing off of the General, raid leader James Andrews gave the order "every man for himself." When the feet of Mark Wood and Alf Wilson hit the ground the Wood County pair could not have imagined what the months ahead would hold for them.

On the Run

Alf Wilson and Mark Wood were in full flight from the General and came to a large, open field. Nearby lay a felled tree, its branches scattered about and there they concealed themselves, the shouts of a pursuing mob filling their ears.

As they lay clutching their revolvers their hearts pounded so hard, "that it seemed to me they could be heard twenty-yards distant," Wilson wrote. Several times their pursuers passed so close they could have touched their legs with their hands. The tension unbearable, Wilson wanted to leap from the pile and open fire, killing as many Southerners as he could before being shot down himself but, "I could not, even in a whisper communicate my wishes to Wood without betraying our place of concealment."

By now the countryside was swarming with soldiers, citizens, and bloodhounds whose baying only added to the terror of the pair. Finally the sun set and it began to rain hard, Wilson and Wood not daring to make a move. They spent all night and the following day laying in water, three or four inches deep at times.

At nightfall the second day, "we were compelled to come out, capture or no capture. We could stand it no longer." Traveling all night in an incessant rain to nearby mountains, daybreak revealed a small barn some distance off the road. They found it to be full of corn fodder and dug themselves holes and fell into an exhausted sleep. That afternoon they were awakened by the voices of two women looking for eggs. One of the women reached in to the hole where Wilson lay, and, as luck would have it, touched his hand.

She let out a scream and threw off the fodder, revealing the two men. She and her friend then sprinted for the house and Wilson and Wood pondered what to do next and "after a moment's thought concluded that the best thing for us to do would be to go to the house and apologize to them and in addition try to get something to eat." They went to the door, bowed, and apologized, explaining they were in pursuit of the raiders and had taken shelter in the barn. The women believed their story and fed them a meal of cornbread and buttermilk.

They continued on, traveling at night for the next two nights and sleeping during the day, eventually coming across a valley dotted with small cabins. Gazing upon the scene, and by

This monument to the Andrews Raiders stands in the Chattanooga National Cemetery in Tennessee. The graves in a semi-circle around the base of the monument are of the eight Andrews Raiders executed in Atlanta. In the far right foreground is the grave of Sergeant John Scott of Findlay, the only northwestern Ohio Raider executed.

now desperately hungry, they fantasized about the different types of food the cabins might contain. They approached one of the cabins and the woman believed their story that they were lost and prepared what was for them a veritable feast of ham and eggs, rye coffee and cornbread. They also learned from her that the town of Cleveland, Tennessee was nearby and there were no soldiers there. After thanking her and paying her some money, they moved on.

They reached Cleveland where Wilson boldly walked into the local bookstore and bought an atlas authored, ironically, by the same General Mitchel who had ordered the raid. They continued on, tearing out the maps they needed and burying the rest, hoping to find Federal lines. Nightfall brought them to another valley and another cabin where a dignified, elderly woman invited them in. They told her they were former Confederate soldiers. She sat them down and prepared some food while maintaining a scrutinizing, skeptical stare, which made them quite uneasy.

Suddenly she turned and said, "You are Union men! You can't fool me! I know a Union man by his look! You need not deny it!" A startled Wilson and Wood were even further surprised when she then said, "I am a Union woman and I am not afraid to own it to anybody. The secessionists around here don't like me a bit for I say just what I think of them, whether they like it or not...I will do anything I can to help you." (There were a considerable number of people in eastern Tennessee who stayed loyal to the Union).

Not sure if it was a trap, Wilson and Wood stuck to their story although she refused to believe them. Meanwhile her elderly husband, who had arrived home while they were eating, gave them information on a safe route. As they left Wilson was tempted to express a bond of Union sympathy and friendship but, being so deep in hostile territory, didn't want to take the chance that their story was a ruse.

They were traveling along the next morning when sharp voice demanded; "Halt or I will blow your brains out." They found themselves surrounded by a large cavalry squad commanded by a captain who said he'd preferred to shoot or hang prisoners rather than take them into custody. Wilson and Wood told the captain they came from local families whose names they had picked up along the way.

As it turned out the captain was familiar with the heads of the families and believed their story. He then accused the two of running away from Southern conscription and even possibly being on their way to join the Union army. He said, "For all I know you may belong to those spies and bridge burners and if I did not know your folks I would send you to Chattanooga under arrest." He then told them they could be freed if they took an oath to the South and Wilson and Wood quickly agreed.

They were taken to the home of a "rank old rebel," given an oath, then endured from the captain and the "hot-tempered" woman of the house "the most fiery lecture on the subject of Southern rights and Northern wrongs we had ever heard." Eventually their revolvers were returned to them and they were allowed to leave.

They returned to the mountains and contemplated their situation. Having been caught once they could not afford to be so caught again. They needed to get to the Tennessee River and get away by boat and decided to go to the house of the couple who had fed them the previous night. Wilson could only hope their expressions of Union loyalty were genuine.

They arrived back at the house late at night and Wilson knocked until the sleeping couple awoke. The husband came to the door and a somewhat awkward exchange followed as each reserved suspicions of the other. Finally Wilson said "Their is no trick in this. I am a Union man in deep trouble, the nature of which I am not just at liberty to mention now." Throughout the conversation, Wilson was aware that the old woman stood in the shadows with a loaded rifle pointed towards his head.

Wilson then asked the old man if he would take a oath to the Union cause and he readily consented. After the oath every one relaxed and Wilson and Wood sat down and told the couple the whole story. They quickly agreed that the pair must not be seen anywhere near the house, for soldiers might be watching. The old man led them to an abandoned house in a secluded area of his farm where a trap door led to a cellar.

There they hid in the dark cellar for several days where the couple brought them food, hidden at the bottom of a basket of corn. They then were taken on a nighttime journey to a tributary of the Tennessee River where a small boat waited. Wilson and Wood were soon swirling downstream in total darkness in a cold, blinding rainstorm. They were now leaving northern Georgia and headed toward Chattanooga, Tennessee.

Before the first gray light of dawn broke, they found an island on which to hide for the day. The rain had changed to sleet and hail and their frozen limbs could barely haul the boat ashore. "I have never, not even in the coldest winter of the North, experienced so much suffering from cold as I did on that terrible night," Wilson wrote.

They sought food and warmth at a cabin on the shore, telling the man there they were with the Confederate Army and on a mission to destroy all the boats in the area to prevent local men from fleeing from conscription. As there had been Confederate soldiers in the area days earlier doing the same thing, their story was believed.

They continued their journey down river, passing through Chattanooga under the cover of darkness and by dawn were well past the city. They now felt their greatest danger was over

Grave of Andrews Raider Mark Wood in Forest Cemetery, Toledo, Ohio.

but the roar of rapids downstream soon told them otherwise. They soon were swirling helplessly through a narrow gorge toward a whirlpool when a log slammed into the boat knocking them past it. They had escaped the whirlpool "no doubt owing to the blow received by the floating log," Wilson wrote.

They now approached more rapids and saw a man on shore frantically waving them over. He said "You are strangers in these parts, aren't you?" He went on to explain that the next rapids were much worse than the ones they had just passed through and that many experienced rivermen had drowned there. Wilson and Wood offered the man three dollars to guide them through and, after much pleading, the man agreed. And, "after a ride I never wish to repeat," wrote Wilson, their boat passed safely through. Their chance meeting with the man probably saved their lives.

They let the man off, paid him, and continued on. Wilson now knew they were approaching territory that lay between the Union and Confederate armies, land which would be heavily patrolled. But which side would they encounter first? Later that day they passed a company of rebel soldiers who yelled at them to pull over but they pretended not to hear and the river was wide enough that they were out of musket range. After that they decided to hide for the day.

The following dawn they pulled over, and learned from locals and fleeing Confederate soldiers that the Union army occupied a nearby town. They ascended a large hill to the town and to their surprise found it swarming with rebel soldiers. The Union troops had merely been on a nighttime raid and had retreated. As it was too late to run, the only thing to do was to remain calm and try to again lie their way out of danger.

At first they weren't noticed then an officer began asking them questions. Things were going pretty well until a local man ran up and accused them of being with the raiding party the night before. They were detained and Wilson began tearing off small pieces of his maps and dropping them on the ground or eating them knowing they would be used against them. They eventually were searched and their revolvers were found and were placed under guard. That night they were taken to nearby town to the commanding officer where they were strip searched and questioned some more.

Suddenly a man ran up and said he knew Wilson and Wood to be Andrews Raiders, that he had seen them on the train. The commanding officer smiled and said, "I'll bet any money, by God, that these are the two men we have been looking after so long." After two weeks on the run Wilson and Wood had, at least for the time being, run out of miracles.

Prison Hell

If life on the run in hostile territory had been rough for Alf Wilson and Mark Wood, things were going to get a whole lot worse. After being incarcerated overnight in a guardhouse surrounded by 50 soldiers, which showed how much the Confederates prized their find, they were transported by train to Chattanooga. "Here our sorrows and hardships began in earnest," Wilson wrote.

Once in Chattanooga they were taken to a prison, handcuffed, and chained together by their necks. They then were led to a room, a trap door was opened, and they were ordered to descend a ladder. As Wilson stepped forward he "caught a breath of the horrible stench and foul hot air which came up through that revolting hole...I had never smelled such a loathsome and sickening smell before."

They clambered down the ladder as well as their chains would permit. It was not until they got to the bottom that they realized that "the stinking, loathsome pit was crowded with miserable human beings smothering and gasping for breath," Wilson wrote. It was pitch dark and so crowded they barely could find a place to stand. Wood County, Ohio never seemed so far away.

The majority of the men in the pit were fellow Raiders. Most of them believed they would soon be hanged and many welcomed the prospect, their condition was so miserable. Also in the 13-foot square hole were a dozen or so civilian prisoners and one escaped slave. [The escaped slave was named Aleck who was seven months into a one-year sentence for escape, Wilson wrote. As he would not say where he had escaped from he was regularly taken out and whipped. He bore his situation without complaint and between beatings even tried to cheer the other prisoners. After his one-year sentence he was to be sold again.]

The conditions in the pit were abominable with bed bugs, fleas and lice of epic proportions. The lice "swarmed our bodies night and day by millions," according to Wilson. Many of the men had open sores and some were nearly naked. The heat in the cell was intense and perspiration constant. There was not enough room for all to lay down at once and many slept leaning against a wall. Food was lowered in a bucket twice a day—cornbread and boiled bacon, the bacon partly spoiled and often with dead maggots. At times local people would come stare down the hole calling the Raiders "Old Abe's abolition dogs," among other epithets.

Wilson's wrists became so swollen from his handcuffs that the iron had sunk into his flesh and could barely be seen. He found that having his elbows tied together brought some relief but this made him helpless against the lice. The cruel confinement of Wilson, Wood and their fellow Raiders lasted several weeks. Then, with Union troops drawing near, the Raiders were taken from their hellhole prison and put on a train for Georgia.

Traveling south along the same rails they had wreaked havoc on about a month previously, the Raiders were greeted at each station by angry and menacing crowds. At Atlanta a furious, swelling mob waited and the train's soldiers surrounded the car and sent for reinforcements. The train finally got underway and "had we been detained fifteen minutes longer we would have been dragged from the cars and hung, or cut to pieces, or beaten to death in the streets..." Wilson wrote.

The train continued on to Madison, Georgia, the jail there representing a major improvement. "We found the jail here to be a paradise compared to our late den at Chattanooga," Wilson wrote. Here they had room, light, fresh air to breathe and decent food. Even though still chained they "soon felt like men again."

After several days stay at Madison, they were returned to Chattanooga as Union forces were no longer threatening the town. But conditions were better in their second stay as a portion were allowed to stay in an upper area, creating more room below. And they had procured a knife which enabled them to release their shackles at times when the guard was not around, thus relieving some of their personal discomfort.

Regarded as spies by the rebels, thus not subject to the typical rules and rights given prisoners of war, death by hanging loomed over the Raiders. At the end of May an officer came and wordlessly handed raid leader James Andrews a letter and walked away. It was his death warrant telling him he had one week to live.

Andrews took the news quietly and calmly. But for the others the message was clear: escape or hang and escaping became an obsession. Using the knife they had secured they began to saw away at the ceiling boards around the trap door. The work was slow and tedious, the blade would get hot and bend at times, and the Raiders would sing hymns to cover up the noise they were making.

Then early one morning they made their attempt at escape and things did not go well. A loosened brick fell to the ground and the sentries were alerted and opened fire. Only Andrews and another man got away. Andrews managed to elude his pursuers for two days, much to the exhilaration of Wilson and the other prisoners. The Raider leader made a heroic effort; without shoes and nearly naked he swam miles in rivers to throw off pursuing dogs but eventually was caught. He was brought back to the prison and thrown down, "chained to the floor, naked, bloody, bruised and speechless, he seemed more dead than alive," Wilson wrote. "His eyes, which were sunken, gave forth a wild, despairing, unnatural light." After a while Andrews recovered enough to speak to his comrades, telling them of his ordeal while providing words of encouragement. He said he knew he would soon die, and regretted that his death would not somehow save their lives.

The Raiders were moved out of the Chattanooga prison again, this time to Atlanta. There on June 7th Andrews was taken away to be executed. He shook hands with each man and was led away, the clinking of his chains the only sound. He was hung from a tree in front a of a cheering crowd, the limb so low his feet touched the ground which left him strangling. "At last someone took a shovel and mercifully removed the earth when he soon expired. The murder was complete," wrote Wilson.

In Atlanta there was one improvement in their conditions. Their chains, which had bound them together in pairs since the beginning of their confinement, were removed. They had worn them so long that at times they would "follow each other about as if still compelled to do so with chains," Wilson wrote. Alf Wilson and Mark Wood had been chained together all this time.

But horror would await them in Atlanta, as they soon would learn. Twelve of the Raiders, who had been sent to Knoxville for trial, were returned. Their fate remained unknown for about a week and hopes rose among the Raiders of a possible parole or a prisoner exchange. Then on June 18th a squad of cavalry arrived at the prison and selected seven of the 12 to be hung immediately.

They were seized and their arms tied, even as they said their farewells. Condemned Raider Sergeant Major Marion Ross

Grave of Andrews Raider John "Alf" Wilson in Union Hill Cemetery northwest of Bowling Green, Ohio.

said, "boys, if any of you ever get back, tell them I died for my country, tell them that I died like a man and did not regret it." Private Samuel Slavens could only stammer "Wife—Children— tell them" before completely breaking down. The seven were then taken out and hung before a jeering mob. One of the executed men was a northwest Ohioan, Sergeant John Scott of Findlay.

The deaths of their fellow Raiders sent Wilson, Wood, and the rest into abject despair. That night they all sat in darkened silence, too overwhelmed with grief to speak. "No pen can describe the anguish of those moments," Wilson wrote.

The Raiders, now numbering 14, spent the rest of a hot and humid Georgia summer in the Atlanta prison. To pass the time they read, formed debating teams, boxed, wrestled, sang songs and hymns and occasionally read newspapers slipped to them by sympathetic black prison workers.

Summer dragged into fall and in early October a guard was overheard saying he expected orders for the execution of the Raiders to come at any time. As the prison they were in was too well constructed to break out, they came up with a desperate plan to seize the jailer when he brought in food, take his keys, surprise and disarm the guards, and scatter into the night.

On the given night (October 16th) the jailer was seized, ironically by a man from Tennessee jailed for his Union loyalties, the cell doors were opened, the guards disarmed, and a mad dash ensued. Alf Wilson was soon in the prison yard running for his life. He made it over the gate and there on the other side was his old running partner, Mark Wood. The two young men from Wood County ran for the forest, bullets slamming into the ground around them, reunited in yet another desperate flight against all odds.

On The Run Again

In comparison to their escape from the train, Wilson and Wood's situation was much more serious. After getting away and hiding in the woods there was an initial feeling of euphoria: "If you have never been in prison as we had been you can never feel the wild, almost childish joy that we miserable beings felt" over being free, Wilson wrote. After that cold reality set in.

Months of imprisonment and terrible food had left them terribly weakened, Mark Wood in particular who had spent much of the time wracked with fever and looked like a skeleton. "His eyes were sunken in his head and seemed to have the wild, unnatural glare of a madman," Wilson wrote. Filthy, their clothes barely rags, and their shoes in poor repair, they looked exactly what they were: escaped and desperate prisoners.

Wilson and Wood knew that any journey north would be too dangerous so they decided to go south, relying on fragmentary recollections of childhood geography. Their goal was the Chattahoochee River and a 300-mile journey to the Gulf of Mexico where perhaps they could reach the Union naval blockade there. They again traveled by night and slept by day, their only food field corn which they gnawed on. Their feet were in terrible condition and pain accompanied every step. Wood's feet were in so much pain that he crawled at times, at one point exclaiming "Alf, what's a fellows life but a curse to him when he has to drag it out this way? I would rather be dead and done with it." But somehow he continued. It got to a point where neither of them felt they could go another mile. Then came the sound of flowing water. They had reached the river. "Desoto did not feel more joy when he first discovered the Mississippi," Wilson wrote.

They quickly found a boat and were on their way. They traveled all night and slept fitfully the next day, tormented by swarms of mosquitoes and vivid dreams of food. That evening they decided they had to get food, by force if necessary. They approached a house of a planter and found an elderly couple home who believed their story that they were Confederate soldiers hungry and broke and invited them in.

Wilson conversed with the old man, speaking with a southern accent and dropping the names of Confederate officers and regiments he had picked up along the way to put on a good front. The man informed him with disgust that the "Yankee raiders" had escaped from the Atlanta prison. "They were a desperate, dangerous lot of scoundrels who ought to have been hung long ago," he said. Wilson and Wood kept eating.

After devouring all the food that was put out, they were on their way. The next several nights were filled with perilous nighttime travel, Wilson at one point being knocked into the river by a ferry rope and the both of them shooting over a dam at "the velocity of an express train." The river kept getting rougher until finally, after reaching a gorge, they had to abandon their boat. This meant a three-day land journey over hills and rocks on empty bellies and excruciatingly painful feet, though they did pick up a little food at two isolated cabins. Wood was so spent that he would reel and stagger as if he were drunk or blind and Wilson at times had to lead him by the hand.

Then came the church spires and smokestacks of a town, Columbus, Georgia, where they knew the river was navigable to the Gulf of Mexico. There they were delayed a couple of days as Wood was unable to walk. Wilson spent the nights looking for a boat and spying on the construction of the gunboat "Muscogee" which was being built in Columbus. They finally got underway in a small, leaky boat then stole another, barely escaping from the owner who saw them pulling away.

Below Columbus the river was wide and navigable with good current and traversed through a remote area of Florida which made detection unlikely. What lift this gave to their spirits was balanced by hunger and swarms of mosquitoes as they traveled at night. They ate field corn and pumpkins they found along shore and draped themselves in Spanish moss to ward off the mosquitoes. "Two more comical-looking beings than we were, thus rigged out, would be hard to find," Wilson wrote. He credited the Chattahoochee mosquitoes for being more voracious than those of the Great Black Swamp back home.

Traveling along they were now regularly encountering two species that life in Wood County had not prepared them for: alligators and water moccasin snakes. They managed to forage a little food at a cabin before Wilson found a vacant cabin with some old fish hooks and line. With no way to make a fire, they caught catfish and ate them raw. Wood ate them like a ravenous wolf, a wild look in his eyes. It had been two weeks since they left Columbus and they had eaten only four meals, supplemented by raw corn and pumpkins.

They continued on and finally neared the coastal city of Apalachicola and the bay of the same name where a Union fleet lay. They passed through the city at night and into the bay, at one point being quite frightened when their boat was surrounded by "monsters [that] would swim on all sides of us with great fins sticking out more than a foot out of the water...one of these fish could have easily wrecked our boat with its huge body. I have never been able to learn to what class these finny monsters belonged," Wilson wrote. [The northwest Ohioans could hardly be blamed for not recognizing a school of dolphins]. They eventually pulled over to sleep, awakening the next morning in a grove of orange, lemon, and palm trees, the likes of which they had never seen before.

Now they faced the danger of taking their small boat into the open waters of the Gulf of Mexico, hoping to find the fleet and safety. Paddling on they eventually sighted what looked to be a small island covered with dead trees. As they drew nearer, the island and trees took the form of a ship's masts and smokestacks. Apprehension turned to pure joy when a breeze revealed the ship's flag to be red, white, and blue.

"We threw down our paddles in the boat and stood up and yelled and screamed and cried like a couple of foolish boys lost in the woods," Wilson wrote. "It now seems like a dream to me—that joyful day—the most joyful of my life." After nearly seven months behind enemy lines, Alf Wilson and Mark Wood were finally safe.

Homeward Bound

But first they had some explaining to do. As they approached a gunboat the commander bellowed, "Who the hell are you and why are you paddling under my guns in this manner for?" Emaciated, dirty, and still draped in Spanish moss, Wilson and Wood looked like anything but soldiers. Wilson did some fast explaining and the two were told to board the ship. As the commander heard more of their story and observed close up their deplorable physical condition, he was moved nearly to tears.

Wilson and Wood were at once fed and allowed to clean up. And as the commander heard of the inhumane treatment of the Andrews Raiders, the angrier he became, erupting "into a swearing frenzy," according to Wilson and sending dispatches to the Navy and War Department advising them of the situation. He wanted Wilson and Wood to stay aboard until they had regained their strength but they wanted to return North as soon as possible in hopes of being able to save their comrades still in prison in Atlanta.

They were given letters of introduction and transferred to a cruiser headed for Key West. They made their way up the east coast via ship, eventually arriving in New York. As they were determined to meet personally with the Secretary of War to update him on the situation of their fellow Raiders they left for Washington D.C. They spent a few days in Baltimore where they told their story to newspaper reporters which led to some celebrity treatment.

In Washington, Wilson set off alone on some matters, forgetting to obtain a pass and promptly was arrested by military guards as the city was under heavy security. Quite exasperated and not knowing who to turn to, he demanded pen and paper with which to write President Lincoln himself.

Mr. President: I have just arrived in the city, fresh from a long imprisonment in Atlanta, Georgia, from which place of confinement I took "French leave."

The Provost Guards have imprisoned me here because I was found without a pass in which I suppose they did but their duty. I know of no officer or friend in the city to whom I can apply for help. Can you do anything for me? If you can, you will greatly oblige your friend.

John A. Wilson
Of the Twenty-First Ohio Volunteer Infantry

No more than a half hour after his message was sent out, Lincoln's personal secretary appeared at the jail and ordered his release. (Lincoln was well aware of who Wilson was from the dispatches sent by the commander of the gunboat).

Now Alf Wilson was on his way to the White House to meet with Lincoln himself. Once there, "the president came forward and took me by the hand, much in the manner a father would on receiving a long lost son," Wilson wrote. Lincoln said "Mr.

Wilson it affords me great pleasure to take you by the hand, and I thank God that your life has been spared." Wilson then met with Lincoln and several aides and told his story, asking that something be done to save the remaining Raiders and Lincoln assured him steps were already underway.

Soon afterward Wilson and Wood left Washington, anxious to rejoin their regiment, the 21st Ohio, which they'd left nine months earlier, catching up to it in Tennessee. There "our old comrades received us as two who had come back from the dead," Wilson wrote. The incredible journey of Alf Wilson and Mark Wood was over.

All the other surviving Raiders made it home safely as well. Six others who escaped from the Atlanta prison along with Wilson and Wood all made it back to Union territory. The remaining six were released via a prisoner exchange in March, 1863.

Both Wilson and Wood served about two more years before being discharged from the service in late 1864. Mark Wood, who was wounded twice in battle after his Andrews Raid adventures, never returned to full health and died in Toledo in 1866 of tuberculosis. John "Alf" Wilson returned to Wood County, was married, and lived most of his life in Haskins. Deteriorating health caused him to apply for invalid pension in 1882 and he died in Perrysburg March 28, 1904. According to a "Perrysburg Journal" article Wilson in the last years of his life, "suffered much, his health never having been good since his terrible experiences in the army." For their service Alf Wilson and Mark Wood, along with the other Andrews Raiders, were awarded the nation's highest military honor, the Congressional Medal of Honor.

CHAPTER XVIII

TALES ALONG THE TRAIL

For an army in the field or on the march, foraging for food was a regular activity when supplies ran low. Foraging, a polite term for stealing, was against regulations which were selectively enforced early in the war and even less so as the war went on. While the 21st Ohio was in Kentucky and on dress parade, the regimental band was ordered to strike up a tune. When the bass drummer did not respond the colonel in charge repeated his order and started to get angry when it was again ignored.

The bass drummer then sidled up to the colonel and quietly informed him that the reason he wasn't playing was because he had a stolen pig hidden inside the drum. Without missing a beat the colonel responded, "Why the hell didn't you tell me you were sick! Go to your quarters." Pork chops, presumably, were on the menu that evening

● ●

It was early in the war and the colonel in command of the 123rd Ohio was reprimanding some of his men for stealing some poultry when an offending captain, of German descent, spoke up in self-defense. "Tam turkey coom'd a runnin out of the gate mit his mouth vide open and Colonel, you don't tink I is goin to let a tam turkey bite me? No sir!

The captain escaped reprimand.

• •

There was a lieutenant with the 111th Ohio who became quite melancholy while stationed in Kentucky and desperately longed for a leave of absence to go home and see his wife and two young children. So he, along with a few of his comrades, devised a plan to obtain a certificate of physical disability from the post surgeon. As he was a strapping man and the picture of health, a set of artificial symptoms would have to be produced.

They decided that a blistered, grotesque-looking tongue and an accelerated pulse would do the trick. First his tongue was scorched with acid and coated with a solution of sulfate zinc. Then to achieve an accelerated pulse he then took 20 grains of quinine, the very bitter-tasting cure for malaria. Most importantly, however, he was advised by his friends to *act* as if ill when he arrived at the surgeon's post.

The lieutenant either forgot his instructions or had no acting skills at all for when he arrived at the surgeon's he strode into the room and threw himself back in his seat. Then with an almost defiant attitude, folded his arms and informed the surgeon he was sick and needed a change of climate.

The surgeon, apparently wise to such schemes, looked him over and declined to check his pulse or examine his tongue. He then told him, "The general expects marching orders soon and that will give you a change of climate all right, but if you should get any worse come down and see me again lieutenant" and walked out of the room. The lieutenant left chagrined and indignant saying the surgeon, "Don't know enough to doctor a dog. Never looked at my tongue or felt my pulse neither. How in the hell could he tell how sick I was?"

But all was not for naught. When then incident got around to the rest of the regiment it created such amusement that the lieutenant forgot his melancholy and "his wanted buoyancy of spirits returned."

• •

Needless to say there was no small degree of animosity between Union troops and citizens of the Confederacy and encounters between the two were often acrimonious. A captain of the 21st Ohio, after being taken prisoner at Chickamauga, was approached by a local citizen who asked him, "What you 'uns come down here to fight we 'uns for?"

"To make you obey the laws of our country," the captain replied. "I'll never obey the laws of a country that treats me as the Lincoln government has," replied the citizen. When the captain asked how he had been treated, he replied that the government had taken all of his livestock and in fact had taken everything he had except his land.

"They didn't serve you right," the captain responded, "they ought to have hung you." The exchange became quite heated after this with citizen telling the captain he would shoot him if he could while the captain shook his fist in his face. When the citizen raised his cane to strike the captain a Confederate guard intervened and dragged him away, telling him that he was a coward and that if he wanted to fight Yankees he should go to the front where he would have all the fighting he wanted.

• •

A private in the 21st Ohio, Jacob Adams of Hancock County, wrote after the war: "I do not know if I ever killed anyone, neither do I want to know, and if I did I would not boast of it. Few soldiers know that they killed an enemy. In action you draw a bead on a man and see him fall as you fire. After the battle you may go to the object you fired at and find he received two or three fatal shots."

• •

While the 37th Ohio was in winter camp in Arkansas in 1864 they did a little exploring, according to a soldier named John Sculenberg. "During our stay there we made a scouting tour along the mountains on the other side of the Tennessee River, the home of the Moonshiners, and spent a few days among them inspecting their stills and the proofs of their highwines which proved strong enough to knock the pins out from under some of the inspectors so much so that they imagined they heard the command 'lay down' and governed themselves accordingly."

Their commanding general came along and seeing this sorry sight, ordered the "inspectors" into line but with limited success. When he was unable to get a man to stand up he "would detail two men to raise the drowsy comrade up to a sitting position and have the men rub his ears with all their might, and if the first application failed to have the desired effect he would order a second which would generally bring them to their feet."

• •

Samuel Linton, of Elmore in Ottawa County, enlisted as a private in the 21st Ohio in August, 1861 and served nearly two years before being discharged due to medical disability from wounds. He kept a journal which included some observations and opinions about slavery.

"We find some very interesting entries in some of the books here. We find that a slave who is sound in limb, mind and body is worth about twelve hundred dollars at the age of 25 to 40. Some would be valued at fourteen hundred. As in the case of Joe and his wife, who had been bought for twenty eight hundred back in years gone by. But on the account of advancing age were marked down to eight hundred. And yet they had been quite profitable to this master. As they had brought forth seven children whose aggregate value was forty two hundred."

"This profit parted husband and wife, parents and children, never to meet again; to teach a slave to read is a penal crime and none dare to interfere on behalf of a slave no matter how inhuman the treatment may be. And this curse must be wiped out or our country shall perish."

"They (slaves) are looked upon by their masters as just as the farmer of the north does his horses. There are kind masters here as well as kind horse owners in the north who will care for their old servant until a natural death relieves them of their charge. When you look around you and see how the different men use their horses, you can then form an idea of how slaves are treated here."

"In years to come it will be very difficult for the people to realize the enormity of the villainies embodied in human slavery. And it will continue to become less real as years go by until this great curse of our nation, which will cost hundreds of thousands of lives and untold suffering and billions in money to wipe out shall become as a fairy tale and like the hanging of witches in years gone by, shall seem as fiction rather [than] true history."

"A political talk came up and got quite warm, Some of the men have friends and relations at home who are democrats of the pro-slavery order and are called by some, home made rebels or copperheads. This has raised the temper of two or three to a white heat and caused them to retaliate by calling the others abolitionist and nigger lovers. I sat by and listened to the holy brethren express themselves in such loving terms and concluded that publicans done as well or even better than those professed children of God. They, because I said so, turned on me and said I was an infidel and a fool. I admitted the last and claimed that I did not disgrace nor anger God as much by my non-belief as they did by their profession. The officer called us down hard and ordered me to keep still, which I did."

ABOUT THE AUTHOR

Jim Mollenkopf is a Toledo, Ohio writer and author who enjoys local history. A former social worker then newspaper reporter, this is his fourth book. He wrote and published *Lake Erie Sojourn: an autumn tour of the parks, public places and history of the Lake Erie shore in 1998; The Great Black Swamp: historical tales of northwest ohio in 1999;* and *The Great Black Swamp II: more historical tales of northwestern ohio* in 2000.

APPENDIX

BATTLES FOUGHT BY THE 21ST OVI

Try Mountain, Kentucky	November 9, 1861
Bowling Green, Kentucky	February 15, 1862
Huntsville, Alabama	April 11, 1862
Bridgeport, Alabama	April 15, 1862
La Vernge, Tennessee	October 7, 1862
Nashville, Tennessee	November 5,1862
Stone River, Tennessee	December 31, 1862 to January 2, 1863
Tullahoma Campaign, Tennessee	June 23-30, 1863
Dug Gap, Georgia	September 11, 1863
Chickamauga, Georgia	September 19-20, 1863
Missionary Ridge, Tennessee	November 25, 1863
Buzzard Roost, Georgia	May 8, 1864
Resaca, Georgia	May 13-16, 1864
New Hope Church, Georgia	May 28, 1864
Kenesaw Mountain, Georgia	June 9-30 1864
Kenesaw Mountain, Georgia (General assault on)	June 27, 1864
Vining Station, Georgia	July 2-5, 1864
Chattahoochee River, Georgia	July 6-19, 1864
Peachtree Creek, Georgia	July 20, 1864
Atlanta Georgia (Hood's first sortie)	July 22, 1864
Jonesboro, Georgia	September 1, 1864
Savannah, Georgia (Siege)	December 10-21, 1864
Averysboro, North Carolina	March 16, 1865
Bentonville, North Carolina	March 19-21, 1865

BATTLES FOUGHT BY THE 111TH OVI

Huff's Ferry, Tennessee	November 14, 1863
Loudon Creek, Tennessee	November 15, 1863
Lenoir, Tennessee	November 15, 1863
Campbell Station, Tennessee	November 16, 1863
Knoxville, Tennessee (Siege of)	November 17 to December 4, 1863
Blain's Crossroads, Tennessee	December 16, 1863
Dandridge, Tennessee	January 16-17, 1864
Buzzard Roost Gap, Georgia	May 8, 1864

Dalton, Georgia	May 9, 1864
Resaca, Georgia	May 13-16, 1864
Dallas, Georgia	May 25 to June 4, 1864
Kenesaw Mountain, Georgia	June 9-30, 1864
Pine Mountain, Georgia	June 14, 1864
Lost Mountain, Georgia	June 16, 1864
Nickajack Creek, Georgia	July 2-5, 1864
Chattahoochee River, Georgia	July 6-10, 1864
Peach Tree Creek, Georgia	July 20, 1864
Atlanta (Siege of)	July 28 to September 2, 1864
Utoy Creek, Georgia	August 5-6, 1864
Lovejoy Station, Georgia	August 31 to September 1, 1864
Columbia, Tennessee	November 24-28, 1864
Franklin, Tennessee	November 30, 1864
Nashville, Tennessee	December 15-16, 1864
Fort Anderson, North Carolina	February 18, 1865
Town Creek, North Carolina	February 20, 1865
Goldsboro, North Carolina	March 21, 1865

Note: Battle listings from "Official Roster of Soldiers of the State of Ohio in the War of the Rebellion."

BATTLES FOUGHT BY BATTERY H, FIRST OHIO LIGHT ARTILLERY

Winchester, Virginia	March 22-23, 1862
Chantily, Virginia	September, 1 1862
Port Republic, Virginia	June 9, 1862
Fredericksburg, Virginia	December 10-12, 1862
Chancellorsville, Virginia	May 2-3, 1863
Gettysburg, Pennsylvania	July 2-3, 1863
Mine Run, Virginia	November 26 to Dec. ?, 1863
Wilderness, Virginia	May 5-7, 1864
Spottsylvania, Virginia	May 8-18, 1864
North Anna River, Virginia at Jericho Mills	May 25-27, 1864
Cold Harbor, Virginia	June 1-2, 1864
Chickahominy, Virginia	June 3-12, 1864
Petersburg, Virginia	June 17-19, 1864

Note: Above according to former battery member Lieutenant William Parmelee as recalled in a 1918 newspaper article.

THE DRUMMER BOY OF MISSION RIDGE

BY KATE BROWNLEE SHERWOOD*

Did ever you hear of the Drummer Boy of Mission Ridge who lay
with his face to the foe 'neath the enemy's guns in the charge of that terrible day?
They were firing above him and firing below and the tempest of shot and shell
was raging like death as he moaned in his pain by the breastworks where he fell.

We had burnished our muskets and filled our canteen as we waited for orders that morn
who knows when the soldier dying of thirst, where the wounded are wailing forlorn.
When forth from the squad that was ordered back from the burst of that furious fire
our Drummer Boy came and his face was aflame with the light of noble desire.

"Go back with your corps," our Colonel had said, but he waited the moment when
he might follow the ranks and shoulder a gun with the best of us bearded men.
And so when the signals from old Fort Wood set an army of veterans wild
he flung down his drum which spun down the hill like the ball of a wayward child.

And so he fell in with the foremost ranks of brave old Company G
as we charged by the flank with our colors ahead and our column closed up like a V.
In the long swinging lines of that splendid advance when the flags of our corps floated out
like the ribbons that dance in the jubilant lines of the march of a gala day rout.

He charged with the ranks though he carried no gun for the Colonel had said nay
and he breasted the blast of the bristling guns and the shock of the sickening fray.
And when by his side they were falling like hail he sprang to a comrade slain
and shouldered his musket and bore it as true as the hand that was dead to pain.

Twas dearly we loved him, or Drummer Boy, with a fire in his bright black eye
that flashed forth a spirit too great for his form, he was only just so high.
As tall perhaps as your little lad who scarcely reached your shoulder
though his heart was the heart of a veteran then, a trifle maybe, the bolder.

He pressed to the front, our lad so leal, and the works were almost won
a moment more and our flags had swung o'er the muzzle of the murderous gun.
But a raking fire swept the van and he fell mid the wounded and the slain
with his wee, wan face turned up to Him who feeleth His children's pain.

Again and again our lines fell back and again with shivering shocks
they flung themselves on the rebel works as the fleet on the jagged rocks.
To be crushed and broken and scattered amain, as the wrecks of the surging storm
where none may rue and none may reck of aught that has human form.

So under the Ridge we were lying for the orders to charge again
and we counted our comrades missing and we counted our comrades slain.
And one said "Johnnie the Drummer Boy is grievously shot and lies
just under he enemy's breastworks; if left on the field he dies."

Then all the blood that was in me surged to up my aching brow
and my heart leaped up like a ball in my throat, I can feel it even now.
And I swore I would bring that boy from the field if God would spare my breath
if all the guns on Mission Ridge should thunder the threat of death.

I crept and crept up the ghastly Ridge by the wounded and the dead
with the moans of my comrades right and left, behind me, and yet ahead.
Till I came to the form of our Drummer Boy in his blouse of dusty blue
with his face to the foe 'neath the enemy's guns where the blast of the battle blew.

And his gaze as he met my own, God wot, would have melted a heart of stone
as he tried like a wounded bird to rise and placed his hand in my own.
So wan and faint with his ruby red blood drank deep by the pitiless sward
while his breast with its fleeting, fluttering breath throbbed painfully slow and hard.

And he said in a voice half smothered, though its whispering thrills me yet
"I think in a moment more I would have stood on the parapet.
For my feet have trodden life's rugged ways and I have been used to climb
where some of the boys have slipped I know but I have never missed a time.

"But now I nevermore will climb and Sergeant when you see
the men go up those breastworks there, just stop and waken me.
For while I cannot make the charge or join in the cheers that rise
I may forget my pain to see the old flag kiss the skies."

Well it was hard to treat him so, his poor limb shattered sore
but I raised him to my shoulder and to the Surgeon bore.
And the boys when they saw us coming each gave a shout of joy
though some in curses clothed their prayers for him, our Drummer Boy.

When sped the news that "Fighting Joe" had saved the Union right
with his legions fresh from Lookout and that Thomas has massed his might.
And forced the rebel centre and our cheering rang like wild
and Sherman's heart was as happy as the heart of a little child.

When Grant from his lofty outlook saw our flags by the hundred fly
along the slopes of Mission Ridge where'er he cast his eye.
And our Drummer Boy heard the news and knew the mighty battle done
the valiant contest ended and the glorious victory won.

Then he smiled in all his agony beneath the Surgeon's steel
and joyed that his blood to flow, his country's woes to heal.
And his bright black eyes so yearning grew strangely glad and wide
I think in that hour of joy he would have gladly died.

And ne'er our ranks again were cheered by our little Drummer's drum
when rub, rub, rub-a dub-dub, we knew that our hour had come.
Beat brisk at morn, beat sharp at eve, rolled long when it called to arms
with a rub, rub, rub-a-dub-dub 'mid the clamor of rude alarms.

Ah, ne'er again our black-eyed boy looked up in the veteran's face
to waken thoughts of his children safe in mother's love embrace.
Oh ne'er again with tripping feet he ran with the other boys
his budding hopes were cast away as they were idle toys.

But ever in our hearts he dwells with a grace that is never old
for him the heart to duty wed can nevermore grow cold.
His heart, the hero's heart we named the loyal true and brave
the heart of the soldiers hoar and gray, of the lad in his Southern grave.

And when they tell of their heroes and the laurels they have won
of the scars they are doomed to carry, of the deeds that they have done.
Of the horror to be biding among the ghastly dead
the gory sod beneath them, the bursting shell o'erhead.

My heart goes back to Mission Ridge and the Drummer Boy who lay
with his face to the foe 'neath the enemy's guns in the charge of that terrible day.
And I say that the land that bears such sons is crowned and dowered with all
the dear God giveth nations to stay them lest they fall.

O glory of Mission Ridge stream on, like the roseate light of morn
on the sons that now are living, on the sons that are yet unborn
And cheers for our comrades living and tears as they pass away
and three times three for the Drummer Boy who fought at the front that day.

---

*Kate Brownlee Sherwood was a Toledoan and much
of her poetry focused on the Civil War. Several volumes of her work were published in the late 1800's.
Her husband, Isaac, was a lieutenant colonel with
the 111th Ohio and finished the war a brevet brigadier general.*

REFERENCES

Adams, Jacob. *Diary of Jacob Adams, Private in Company F, 21st O.V.V.I.* Columbus: Herr Printing Co., 1930.

Austin, James C. *Petroleum V. Nasby.* New York: Twayne Publishers Inc., 1965.

Barbiere, Joe. *Scraps From the Prison Table at Camp Chase and Johnson's Island.* Doylestown, PA: W.W.H. Davis, Printer: 1868.

Beath, Robert B. *History of the Grand Army of the Republic.* New York: Bryan, Taylor & Co., 1888.

Boatner, Mark M. *The Civil War Dictionary.* New York: David McKay Co., 1959.

Breen, Donald J. *The History of the Federal Civil War Prison on Johnson's Island, Ohio, 1862-1865.* Thesis (M.A.) Kent State University, 1962.

Canfield, S.S. *History of the 21st Regiment Ohio Volunteer Infantry in the War of the Rebellion.* Toledo: Vrooman, Anderson & Bateman, Printers, 1893.

Cleaves, Freeman. *Rock of Chickamauga.* Norman: University of Oklahoma Press, 1948.

Clemens, Cyril. *Petroleum Vesuvius Nasby.* International Mark Twain Society, 1936.

Dority, Orin "The Civil War Diary of Orin G. Dority." (Parts 1 & 2) *Northwest Ohio Quarterly,* 37 (Winter 1964-65 and Summer 1965) 7-26 and 104-115.

Elderbrock, Stephen W. *The Emergence of Petroleum Vesuvius Nasby.* Thesis No. 6330 (M.A.) Bowling Green State University, 1994.

Fox, William F. *Regimental Losses in the American Civil War.* Albany, NY. Brandow Printing Co., 1898.

Frohman, Charles E. *Rebels on Lake Erie.* The Ohio Historical Society, 1965.

Furgurson, Ernest B. *Chancellorsville 1863.* New York: Alfred A. Knopf, 1992.

Garner, Marcia. *Every Care and Kindness.* Thesis No. 186 (M.A.) The University of Toledo, 1996.

Gladieux, Rolland J. *Battery H: The 1st Ohio Light Artillery in Virginia, 1864-65.* Eggertsville, NY: The Buffalo Printing Co.,

1982.

Hannon, Kyle. "Passing the Time: Prison Life at Johnson's Island." *Northwest Ohio Quarterly,* 66 (Spring, 1994) 82-102.

Harper, Robert S. *Ohio Handbook of the Civil War.* Columbus: The Ohio Historical Society, 1961.

Harrison, John M. *The Man Who Made Nasby, David Ross Locke.* Chapel Hill: The University of North Carolina Press, 1969.

Harrison, John M. *The Blade of Toledo.* Toledo: The Toledo Blade Co., 1985.

Hatcher, Harlan. *Lake Erie.* New York: Bobbs-Merrill Co., 1945.

Hoogenboom, Ari A. *Rutherford B. Hayes: Warrior and President.* Lawrence: University of Kansas Press, 1995.

Horowitz, Robert F. *James M. Ashley: A Biography.* Thesis (Ph.D) The City University of New York, 1973.

Hubbel, John T. "A Bright Particular Star: James Birdseye McPherson." *Timeline* (August-September, 1988) 32-45.

Kaser, James A. *At the Bivouac of Memory.* New York: Peter Lang Publishing Co., 1996.

Knauss, William H. *The Story of Camp Chase.* Nashville: Publishing House of the Methodist Episcopal Church, 1906.

Linton Samuel. *The Civil War Diary of Samuel A. Linton.* NP.

Locke, David Ross. *The Struggles of Petroleum V. Nasby.* Toledo: Locke Publishing Co., 1880.

Lupien, David L. *Our Boys Who Wore the Blue.* NP. 1985.

Marchman, Watt P. *The Story of a President: Rutherford B. Hayes and Spiegel Grove.* Fremont: The Rutherford B. Hayes Presidential Center, 1988.

McDonough, James L. and Jones, James P. *War So Terrible: Sherman and Atlanta.* New York: W.W. Norton & Co., 1987.

McElroy, Joseph C. *Chickamauga: Record of the Ohio Chickamauga and Chattanooga National Park Commission.* Cincinnati: Earhart and Richardson, Printers and Engravers, 1896.

Miller Charles C. *A History of Allen County, Ohio.* Chicago: Richmond and Arnold, 1906.

Morgan, John M. *James M. Ashley and Emancipation.* Thesis (M.A.) The University of Toledo, 1949.

Morgan, John M. "Old Steady: The Role of General James Blair Steedman at the Battle of Chickamauga." *Northwest Ohio*

Quarterly, 22 (Spring, 1950) 72-94.

O'Neil, Charles. *Wild Train: The Story of the Andrews Raiders.* New York: Random House, 1956.

Patterson, Edmund DeWitt. *Yankee Rebel: The Civil War Journal of Edmund DeWitt Patterson.* John G. Barrett (ed.) Chapel Hill: The University of North Carolina Press, 1966.

Pittenger, William. *The Great Locomotive Chase.* Philadelphia: The Penn Publishing Co., 1929.

Ransome, Jack C. *The Career of David Ross Locke and its Significance.* Thesis (M.A.) The University of Toledo, 1947.

Reid, Whitelaw. *Ohio in the War.* Cincinnati: The Robert Clark Co., 1895.

Reynolds, Charles E. "Thirteen Months at Andersonville Prison and What I Saw There." *Northwest Ohio Quarterly*, 27 (Summer, 1955) 94-113.

Ryall, Lydia. *Sketches and Stories of the Lake Erie Islands.* Norwalk, Ohio: The American Publishers Co., 1913.

Ryan, Daniel J. *The Civil War Literature of Ohio.* Cleveland: The Burrows Brothers Co., 1911.

Scribner, Harvey. *Memoirs of Lucas County and the City of Toledo.* Madison WI: Western Historical Association, 1910.

Sherwood, Kate Brownlee. *Camp-Fire, Memorial Day, and Other Poems.* Chicago: Jansen, McClurg & Co., 1885.

Sherwood, Isaac R. *Souvenir...One Hundred Eleventh O.V.I.* Toledo: B. F. Wade, Printers, 1907.

Shriver, Phillip R. and Breen, Donald J. *Ohio's Military Prisons in the Civil War.* Columbus: Ohio State University Press, 1964.

Slocum, Charles E. *History of the Maumee River Basin.* Defiance, OH, NP, 1905.

Thurstin, Wesley S. *History of the One Hundred and Eleventh Regiment O.V.I.* Toledo: Vrooman, Anderson & Batemen, Printers, 1894.

Tucker, Glenn. *Chickamauga: Bloody Battle of the West.* New York: Bobbs Merrill Co., 1961.

Vance, William J. "On Thomas' Right at Chickamauga" *Blue and Gray*. (February, 1893) 87-99.

Van Tassel, Charles S. *Story of the Maumee Valley, Toledo and Sandusky Region.* (V. 1) Chicago: S. J. Clarke Publishing Co.,

1929.

Waggoner, Clark. *History of Toledo and Lucas County.* New York and Toledo: Munsell & Co., 1888.

Ward, Geoffrey C. et al. *The Civil War.* New York: Alfred A. Knopf, 1990.

Whaley, Elizabeth J. *Forgotten Hero: General James B. McPherson.* New York: Exposition Press, 1955.

Williams, T. Harry. *Hayes of the Twenty-Third.* Lincoln: University of Nebraska Press, 1965.

Wilson, John A. *Adventures of Alf Wilson.* Toledo: Blade Printing & Paper Co.,1880.

Woods, J.T. *Steedman and His Men at Chickamauga.* Toledo: Blade Printing and Paper Co., 1876.

Yeager, Raymond. *A Critical Analysis of the Anti-Slavery Speeches of Representative James Ashley.* Thesis (M.A) Bowling Green State University, 1950.

_____*A Standard History of Allen County, Ohio.* New York: The American Historical Society, 1921.

_____*History of Allen County, Ohio.* Chicago: Warner, Beers & Co., 1885.

_____*History of Defiance County, Ohio.* Chicago: Warner, Beers & Co., 1883.

_____*Official Roster of the Soldiers of the State of Ohio in the War of the Rebellion V 3,8,10.* Cincinnati: The Ohio Valley Press, 1888.

_____*Report of the Gettysburg Memorial Commission.* Columbus: Press of Nitshke Bros., 1887.

_____*The Allen County Reporter.* V. LIII, No. 1-2. Allen County Historical Society, 1997.

_____*The Columbia Book of Civil War Poetry.* Richard Marius (ed.) New York: Columbia University Press, 1994.

_____*Touched by Fire: A Photographic Portrait of the Civil War.* V 1.William C. Davis (ed.) Boston: Little, Brown and Co., 1985.

Newspaper Articles
Lima Weekly Gazette, April 24, 1861.

"Casualties in the 14th Ohio—None Killed." *Toledo Daily Blade,* September 25, 1863.

David Ross Locke, "Nasby" Personal Tributes." *Toledo Daily*

Blade, February 15, 1888.

"Unveiled The Painting." *Toledo Daily Blade,* March 14, 1894.

"General John S. Kountz, Drummer and Commander." *Toledo Daily Blade,* September 3, 1908.

"Famous Mitchel Raider Joins the Great Silent Army on the Other Shore." *Perrysburg Journal,* April 1, 1904.

"Civil War Hero Answers Call." *Toledo Daily Blade,* June 14, 1909.

"Sketches and Items of Interest on Huntington's Battery Co. H 1st Ohio Light Artillery." *Marietta Sunday Observer,* September 1, 1918.

"Toledo's Civil War Tiger." *The Blade,* June 26, 1966.

"After The Civil War, Dedication to Peace." *The Blade,* July 3, 1966.